THE MEANING OF MISSION

ORBIS BOOKS
Maryknoll, New York 10545

THE
MEANING
OF
MISSION

Jesus, Christians,
and the Wayfaring Church

JOSEPH COMBLIN

TRANSLATED BY JOHN DRURY

Originally published as "Atualidade da Teologia da Missão" in *Revista Eclesiástica Brasileira*, December 1972, March 1973, and September 1973. The English translation is based on the Spanish version: *Teología de la misión*, published by Centro de Estudios Teológicos, Talca, Chile

---

Library of Congress Cataloging in Publication Data

Comblin, Joseph, 1923-
    The meaning of mission.

    Translation of Teología de la misión.
    1. Mission of the church. 2. Missions—Theory.
I. Title.
BV601.8.C6513   266   76-41723
ISBN 0-88344-304-X

CONTENTS

CONTEMPORARY RELEVANCE OF THE THEOLOGY OF GOSPEL MISSION

For many reasons I am inclined to think that today the theology of the Gospel mission is the central issue where the major controversies among Christians converge. My feeling is that many of the concepts and theses and arguments dividing factions within the Church just do not get to the root of the matter. There is no progress because the adversaries do not make explicit the basic conceptions that underlie their points of dis-agreement. They do not make explicit the suppositions that lie behind their line of argument. And if we explore what lies implicit in their explicit remarks, if we try to pinpoint the theology that underlies their pastoral options, we soon discover that they have different interpretations of the Gospel mission.

The fact is that the theology of the Gospel mission has not yet been developed and spelled out satisfactorily. We cannot hope to find it simply by having recourse to published books and articles. In the past thirty years we have seen the rise of many worthwhile and forward-looking missionary initiatives in the Church. This has been particularly true in Brazil in recent years, for example. There communities, movements, and missionary groups have formed to work out a new Christian *modus operandi* in the world. (It is often described as a new "pastoral" effort, though that may not be the most felicitous term.)

It cannot be said, however, that these new efforts have been matched by a corresponding effort in the realm of theological conceptualization. To be sure, we must not exaggerate the importance of theology in the Church and in mission work. Earlier workers and real missionaries have not needed theology in order to carry out their efforts and search for new approaches. The necessary enlightenment and guidance has come from the Gospel message, from the inspiration of the Spirit in scrutinizing the signs of the times and relating them to the biblical texts, and from the support of enlightened members of the hierarchy.

1. Historical Background

Theology is a reflective action, a process undertaken on the basis of prior experiences. The concrete element of missionary praxis will always be prior to the theology, and the latter must always take the former into account. If theology does not do that, if it makes no reference to concrete actions, then it is empty talk of use to no one. It will merely repeat the literal words of the Bible or tradition. That may be fine for studying the history of Christian doctrine or the history of theology, but in itself it is not theologizing.

But there comes a point when we must make explicit our experience of the Gospel mission, when we must examine it critically and synthesize it in carefully worked out concepts. This obligation is not properly that of missionaries, but of the Church itself. The Church must interpret what exactly is going on in the mission experience, appraising the import and scope of its novel features. It must try to comprehend the signs of the times offered by that experience. To do that, the Church must go back to its sources, reread its texts, and critically re-examine its past traditions that may have been unwittingly canonized. The Church must rework its theology in the light of experience, undergoing conversion if that is required.

But our theology of the Gospel mission is inadequate. Its content up to now can be summarized under a few basic themes and heads. There is the segment known as "missiology," which up to now has remained on the margins of theology. It is concerned with the tasks of "missionaries," but it defines that field in a very specific and narrow sense. "Missionaries" are the men and women in religious orders who labor in regions under the control of the Roman Congregations concerned with missions or the propagation of the faith. Until a few years ago missiology was merely an applied version of ecclesiology designed to provide this missionary personnel with a suitable ideology for their work. By very definition "missiology" is not concerned with the vast majority in the Church. It is a body of doctrine for specialized groups. The theologians did not pay much attention to missiology, and the great issues discussed by them were not the problems confronted by missionaries.

The most representative work in the field of missiology is probably the classic by Thomas Ohm: *Machet zu Jüngern alle Völker* (Fribourg: Erich Wavel, 1961).Vatican II attempted to integrate missiology into the more general framework and concepts of theology, to move it out of its traditional isolation. But even Vatican II deemed it wise to publish a special document on the subject with its own distinctive theological basis, thus acknowledging that ecclesiology itself is not sufficiently missionary, that it does not pay sufficient attention to the proclamation of the Gospel message among all the peoples of the world.

After World War II, two movements converged to fashion a new and distinctive missionary perspective. The convergence itself was almost by chance, as explorations in biblical theology were paralleled by the growing realization that Western society itself was becoming dechristianized. On the one hand, biblical theology was obliged to pay more attention to the theme of Gospel mission than ordinary theology was wont to do. On the other hand, the dechristianization process forced the Church to view its whole pastoral effort from a more "missionary" standpoint. All the regions that had been part of the cultural system known as Christendom would now have to be regarded as "mission lands" by the Church, and people began looking around for a theology that would fit in with this new outlook. It was the era of the periodical *Parole et Mission,* and its ideology is embodied in the books of A.M. Henry.

In fact, however, this "mission-oriented" Church had not changed radically at all. Its institutions remained those that had characterized the cultural reality known as Christendom. Pastors of good will tried to adapt those institutions to missionary ends, and others attempted to revise ecclesiology by applying the traditional topics to missionary ends. But the "missionary parish" and the "missionary liturgy" and "missionary evangelization" really came down to the same old parish, the same old liturgy, and the same old catechesis with new names. The themes of biblical theology relating to the Gospel mission were simply applied to the traditional ecclesiastical institutions. The "new" missionary theology was designed to revitalize the prestige of age-old institutions that had been called into question by the process of dechristianization within cultural Christendom.

Up until quite recently most church officials felt that the present-day challenge could be met simply by modernizing and cleaning up the facade of Christian and Catholic institutions. In their view there was no need to replace them with new institutions. A change in terminology and vocabulary was seen as one way to effect this renovation. If one took the themes of biblical theology and applied them to long-standing ecclesiastical traditions, perhaps that alone would be enough to breathe new life into them. And so a host of traditional items were garbed in new terminological dress. People began to talk about "evangelization," "witness," "word," "sign," "community," "commitment," "service," "poverty," and so forth. But how could one really take an institution that had been designed to "command" and ask it to "serve"? How could one effect such a change in such institutions as the parish, the diocese, and the papacy? There was really only one way to do it, and that was to empty the notion of service of any meaningful content. "Service" would simply mean "administration." It would mean almost the same thing that is implied in such terms as public service, social service, health service, tax service. Now there is nothing wrong with that use of the word, but it is not at all what the Bible has in mind when it talks about "service." The Gospel message is trying to say something very different.

Here is another instance where we are faced with the problem of what the Bible really means to Christians. Vatican II reiterated the age-old doctrine in excellent terms, but it is a doctrine that is never given practical application. The Bible is normative. It is not supposed to conform to human beings; they are supposed to conform to it. We should not try to force the Bible to conform to what the Church of today is saying and doing. Instead we should compel the Church of today to conform to what the Bible is saying. But preachers usually take the easy way out. The usual homiletic approach is to hunt through the Bible to find texts that will justify the existing situation, the present *modus operandi*, the traditional lines of conduct, and the age-old institutional forms. Exegesis proves fruitless because it has been decided what the practical application will be before we even start. We know that the Bible will be used to endorse everything that our present-day Church is already doing.

The correct approach is exactly the opposite. We have

to go back and look at the Bible because we know that countless aspects of the life of the Church and present-day Christians have little or nothing to do with Jesus Christ at all. They are the product of the past, of popular traditions, of concessions made to weak sinners over the course of history. We must submit all that to the judgment of God's revealed word. We must change what does not conform with God's will and give form and shape to the plan God seeks to implement. We must read the Bible with an unprejudiced mind, prepared to correct everything that stands in need of correction.

It is in this frame of mind that people are now trying to formulate a new theology of the Gospel mission. From the viewpoint of the Bible, we do not have to change what was written and explicitated in a previous generation. Our task now is to submit the questions and problems of today to the judgment of the biblical text.

First of all, we must recognize that in the framework of the Gospel message itself the basic theme of Gospel mission is not a secondary one alongside many others. Rather, it is the basic, fundamental theme giving rise to all the rest and shedding light on them. We must fashion a theological synthesis that will make that point clear and give it its proper stress.

Secondly, we must realize that all crucial questions of our own day must be viewed in the light of the basic theme of the Gospel misssion. And if we are not inclined to rely on mere sentiment or to cling to peace of mind at any price, we can readily see the great questions facing Christians today. What is the function of the Church? Why should one be Christian? Does it make any sense to form a Church? What are the purposes and goals and governing criteria behind the activity of the Church?

Today the Gospel mission is the only standpoint that furnishes us with a solid starting point. We all realize that the Church with which we are familiar is no longer a solid starting point. Indeed that Church is actually the point at issue and the problem.

At the start I said that the theology of the Gospel mission is the central issue toward which many current Christian controversies converge. Some specific examples might bring out that point more clearly.

2. Major Tensions in Contemporary Christianity

First and foremost among the problems considered by any theology of the Gospel mission is that of the proper *goals of mission* and the general orientation and direction dictated by those goals. There are two basic ways of viewing the Gospel mission. The first way views this mission as the expansion and increase of the groups that are visibly integrated into the institutional forms of the existing Church. Missionary activity comes down to recruiting new members into the Church, increasing its adherents, and adding to its prestige and social influence. The spoken word is used to argue, convince, and attract people to the Church. Some who take this approach would focus on the "gentle" pressure of family and friends, some would go further and use the less gentle pressure of social and political authorities, and still others would make an effort to organize this pressure by bringing it to bear on those segments of society most sensitive to social pressures—e.g., young people, women, the aged, and infirm. Now all that can be well and good. Indeed such institutions might be justified by reasons which have no taint of proselytism in them. The point is that in such an approach pastoral activity centers around the administration of the Church and its affairs, and the Gospel mission is an ancillary activity designed to bolster the expansion and strength of the organism being administered.

Needless to say, few people would describe their pastoral activity in those terms. But the fact is that most church activities and structures, even in so-called mission lands, are designed to abet the administration, consolidation, and expansion of what is already in existence. Those still outside the Church are asked to join those who have already been integrated into the Church. They are asked to adopt the Church's pattern of conduct, to imitate those who are Christians already. Indeed there is no real need to ask them outright, for the approach is clear enough and words are scarcely necessary.

It need hardly be pointed out that this mission method has proved to be totally ineffective, totally incapable of effecting the desired conversions. For more than two hundred years people have been leaving the Church, and relatively few people are moving in the opposite direction, aside from some culturally primitive ones. Millions have left the Church whereas only thousands have entered. But still the Church goes on, thanks to natural increase among its members. The Church is reproducing not by virtue of evangelization or mission work but by virtue of nature and biology, just as ancient Israel did. When all is said and done, it seems that the Church can go on living without undertaking the Gospel mission, that it need only continue to administer the flock nature provides it. But that does raise a crucial question: How do we reconcile that approach with the New Testament?

The second view of the Gospel mission does not start with the Church but rather with Christ himself. It sees the Gospel mission as an imitation and renewal of his

mission. After all, wasn't that the inspiration underlying the great charismatic figures and reform movements of the past? Wasn't that what inspired Francis and
Dominic and Bernard and Ignatius and a host of others?
Jesus addressed himself to those who were outside. He
spoke to denounce and announce, to provoke a transformation in people's lives, to liberate people from the
dead weight of the past, the synagogue, the scribes, and
the traditional outlook. The Church comes after the
Gospel mission, not before it. The privileged objects of
the Gospel mission are the lost sheep: publicans, sinners, prostitutes, lowly Galileans, and many others of
that ilk. The evangelists stress this point over and over
again, and the missionary activities of the disciples take
their inspiration from the activities of Jesus himself: his
teaching approach, his gestures, his social behavior, and
his public attitudes.

The difference between these two views of the Gospel
mission is a radical one. The first operates in terms of
those who are inside while the second operates in terms
of those who are outside. The first looks for visible results, primarily quantitative and only secondarily qual-
itative; the second is concerned with quality rather than
with quantity, and it does not try to take an inventory of
results. The first tries to integrate people into homogeneous molds and thus create uniformity; the second
does not have any a priori molds or models and it provokes diversity.

It should be pointed out that the two approaches are
not mutually exclusive by any means. But the fact remains that one or the other will be stressed, thus giving
overall shape to the Church's effort. Spontaneous tendencies lead people toward the first approach, by virtue
of sociological determinisms. The second approach results from a deliberate decision made in the face of the
prevailing currents.

What does the theology of the Gospel mission have to tell us? Is the work of the Church to carry on and revitalize what Jesus himself did, incarnating it in each new cultural context? Or are we to assume that Jesus did what he did to save us the effort, so that we need only hoard and preserve the capital he accumulated and disburse the spiritual treasures he gained for us? Did Jesus found and organize the Church so that we need only administer it today?

A second major tension concerns the *relationship between Christianity and the world* (which would include the Church-world issue). Here again there are two ways of viewing the matter, one static and the other dynamic. The static view is the more common one. So self-evident is it to many people that they regard it as the most characteristic feature of Christianity itself. In this view the Church and the world are two complete, parallel totalities existing alongside each other. Both are "perfect societies," as Bellarmine put it (though in a different context). Each has its own distinctive course of growth and development, based on its own distinctive values and ends. Each operates in its own order, which is different from that of the other. The Church operates in the "religious" or "moral" or "spiritual" order whereas the world operates in the "temporal" or "profane" order. There is much contact and involvement between the two, and there is certainly room for collaboration, solidarity, dialogue, and service—to use the terms of Vatican II. (These terms are spiritual in inspiration, and they were proposed to correct the excessively juridical outlook of previous centuries.) This being the case, the Church tries to maintain the best possible relationship with the world. (In this respect Vatican II seems to have been very optimistic, and current theology is reversing that approach at a fast pace.) Yet despite the room left open for dialogue, collaboration, and service, the fact remains that all this is secondary in the Church. It has its own mission to carry out in a distinct order that is just as real and self-contained as that of the world. So the Church really carries out two kinds of activity. One is its major activity within its own proper order; the other is very important but still secondary, and it is carried out in the order of the world, which is not really the Church's home ground.

This dualistic view has brought critical reactions from many people, but they often do not question the underlying schema at all. Instead they simply try to get the Church more and more involved in the temporal order and to make this involvement a significant factor. That is enough to raise cries of alarm and accusations of "horizontalism." Debate over "horizontalism" and "verticalism" seems unavoidable. At the very least one must be constantly concerned with the matter, if for no other reason than to avoid being accused of one or the other.

The second view rejects the static schema of two separate worlds or totalities or orders. It points out that the notion of two orders or realms came to center stage in the theology of the sixteenth century, that it was of Protestant inspiration. The doctrine of the two realms was a key point in the theology of Luther, which Catholics accepted under different terms. But this doctrine was unknown in the early Church and the Middle Ages. While some regarded it as an advance, others saw it as a step backward.

The second view under discussion here does not accept the existence of two orders or realms. The mission of Jesus does not constitute a separate, self-contained order alongside that of the world. It is precisely a mission, that is, a movement. It is not another world but a movement for the sake of this world. Jesus comes into this world and goes to work on it. Any attempt to define Christianity in static terms destroys its essential features and creates insoluble dilemmas.

Jesus Christ addressed himself to the whole of this world, to each individual being in it and to the world as a totality. He did not propose or live some parallel existence alongside the world; instead he embodied a way of acting in the world. His mission represents a way of living in this world that is designed to penetrate and transform everything. Christ plunged into the world to alter it by his mission. Christ is a movement, a line of action. He does not proceed from the world but he does live in this concrete, profane world. When he tells us that he will be present wherever two or three are gathered in his name, he is not talking about a reunion in some juxtaposed spiritual realm; he is talking about a reunion anywhere in this real world. Thus the distinction between Christ and the world is not a distinction between two orders. It is distinction between the spoken message and the person who hears it, between the gesture made and the person who perceives that gesture, between the blowing wind and the solid earth (for the Apocalypse says that Christ is Spirit). Just as Christ does not stay on the sidelines outside the world, so those who carry on his work are plunged into the world. But they are not dominated or driven by the world; instead they work to shape and transform it.

Here again we are forced to choose between two different viewpoints. What does the Gospel say?

The third major problem has to do with *the content of salvation and its historicity*. One line of theological thinking, supported by important names in present-day theological circles, views salvation as an invisible mystery of communion with God. This expression sums up all the New Testament themes concerning our relationship with God: children of God, body of Christ, people of

God, and so forth. All these notions point to a select gathering with no reference to history whatsoever. Salvation will attain its full measure in the future life. In this world it is a secret, invisible, interior life that accompanies the concrete lives of Christians and gives meaning to their existence; but it does not enter into temporal life itself, into the life of the body and the mind. The worldly life of the Christian follows the same course as that of other human beings who are not Christians.

Historicity, then, remains totally external to salvation, to the kingdom of God that is mysteriously present in some way. In every age Christians are faced with the problem of determining how to live a truly Christian way of life, how to salvage their faith and remain loyal to God in the midst of the world. The historicity of Christianity comes down to the fact that the Christian way of life must react to all the changes in human cultures and civilizations. Historical activity comes from the external world into the Christian world, but of course it does not affect anything essential in the latter. It merely affects it on the superficial level of adaptation to the surrounding environment. Historicity does not affect the Church itself or Christian doctrine, for they are supratemporal realities; it merely affects the credibility of the Church and its doctrine. Grace and salvation elevate us to a higher order of communion with God. Insofar as human life is elevated to that order, it enters a realm of tranquillity and immutability.

In the second view, salvation takes the sin of the world as its starting point. The world as a totality, both individual and societal life, is under the domination of sin. And sin must be considered in all its historical reality, in all its varied forms of domination, exploitation, and human egotism. Salvation entails a radical change in humanity, but not in a sudden fell swoop of magic from the outside. The change must come about through awakening the human heart to freedom and love. In its initial stage this salvation can be regarded as a seed or a sudden stimulus to life that must be constantly kept alive and is ever in danger from hostile forces. Divine sonship, the body of Christ, and the people of God are not mysterious entities above and beyond ordinary human life. They are essentially dynamic movements, existing only as part of our continuing effort to capture and recapture our full measure of humanity. Outside of this ongoing movement we find only illusion or religious myth.

Salvation, then, is thoroughly conditioned by historical circumstances. It is concrete, just as sin is. Its object is always unique and well defined by the circumstances in which we find ourselves. It is as narrow and as broad as the sinfulness of the world itself. That sinfulness, for all its range and depth, is made up of a multitude of individual forms of cowardice and egotism. Salvation is simultaneously an individual action and a social action. Its effect is not to elevate us to some atemporal order but rather to bring about our transformation. Membership in the body of Christ is the origin and source of salvation, not its end result. The dynamic thrust of salvation moves from Christianity to the world.

According to the first viewpoint, Christians live their lives preoccupied with the necessity of preserving their faith in the midst of a threatening world. According to the second viewpoint, living Christians are ever preoccupied with the sin in the world because their life is based on faith. In the first viewpoint Christ is the object that Christians try to keep before their eyes; in the second viewpoint Christ lives in and through Christians so that they may ever look at the world with Christ's own outlook.

The fourth major tension has to do with *the starting point of theology,* and here again we find two basic points of view. The first remains faithful to the theological vision that dominated the cultural system known as Christendom. It takes as its starting point the concept of divine revelation. All the aspects and elements of Christianity are viewed as part of a divine revelation, as part of a divine doctrine. Christian theological science looks at Christianity with an objective gaze, as if it were an object for contemplation. Christianity is viewed as a complete and self-contained object, and progress in understanding it is viewed as a purely intellectual task. This choice of a starting point and this way of organizing theology is modelled after the approach of Greek philosophy, as the theologians of Christendom themselves admit.

This being the case, it is obvious that the progress and elaboration of theology will have nothing to do with the conflicts, tensions, and anxious searching of the world on the one hand, or with the pastoral experiences and initiatives of the Church on the other hand. There is no way we can expect such a theology to provide guidance for our concrete lives and praxis. From the standpoint of Greek philosophy concrete life and praxis come under the heading of the empirical arts; it is not an object of scientific or scholarly philosophy, because it is not a worthy object of such reflection. Philosophical reflection contemplates the mirror image of eternity in the essences of things. The Christian version of theology that took revelation as its starting point and that dominated cultural Christendom was a theology that contemplated eternal essences. It took for granted that the essential aspect of Christianity was that which was immutable, that which mirrored the eternal.

But another and different starting point is possible, i.e., the concept of mission. The very being and ongoing life of Jesus is his mission, and everything comes under that basic heading. The Bible tells us that there is another type of knowledge and understanding outside the epistemological forms peculiar to specific human cultures.

The knowledge and understanding of Jesus and his disciples is attained and experienced concretely in their mission work. Only those who operate in the context of this mission perspective can really know God and the things of God. It is in mission work that this gift is granted to them. Those who remain outside that perspective cannot grasp the essential, for knowledge comes from action, not contemplation. Defining the essences of divinely revealed objects is not the basic task of theology because those essences lie beyond us. The basic problem for theology can be summed up in such questions as these: How can one be a Christian today? What would Christ do if he were here today? How are we to interpret the present moment?

Any other abstract science or discipline will only disappoint and mislead us. The various objects of what is called "divine revelation" must be framed within the context of the questions we have just asked, for only then can they offer any help to the Christian way of life. If we want to grasp the significance of such realities as God, the Spirit, the Church, sin, salvation, and eschatology, then we must consider them in the context of Christ's mission. If we do not take mission as our starting point, then theology will never get down to the basic question: What are we to do today? Since our conclusion and approach is virtually included in our starting point, it is important to choose the right starting point.

3. The Mission of Jesus Christ

My purpose here is to trace the general outlines of a theology of the Gospel mission. I shall merely spell out the basic biblical data in a succinct way. Those who want a more detailed treatment can have recourse to the many dictionaries and treatises of biblical theology that carry out the task admirably. Here I shall not go over the whole ground covered by those works. I shall simply discuss some of the more important and well-known biblical texts that have to do with our theme.

The fact is that expositive theology pays relatively little attention to the aspect of the biblical message that I regard as most important in our present circumstances. So in the following paragraphs I shall try to provide a brief summary of the New Testament passages that deal with the mission of Jesus, regarding them as the proper basis of any theology of the Gospel mission.

When Jesus talks about himself, he describes himself as an "envoy," as one who has been sent. He tells us that he has come to do a certain thing or that the Father has sent him to do something. He does not provide his friends or disciples with much information concerning his inner life, his character, or other things that we commonly associate with an individual's personality. His personality is described in terms of his mission, is identified with that mission. For Jesus his mission is not just a function or a task or a profession; it envelops and occupies his whole being and life.

In the synoptic Gospels Jesus has little to say about himself, and so the little he does have to say in that connection is noteworthy: "Let us move on to the neighboring villages so that I may proclaim the good news there also. That is what I have come to do" (Mark 1:38). The fourth Gospel, by contrast, focuses our attention on the person of Jesus. And in its account Jesus appeals to his mission no less than forty times. Various forms of the verbs "come" and "send" occur again and again. Here are two sample texts: "I was sent by One who has the right to send. . . . I know him because it is from him I come; he sent me" (John 7:28–29); "as you have sent me into the world, so I have sent them into the world" (John 17:18).

At a later date, when the apostles and New Testament writers attempt to sum up the whole happening in a few words, they are compelled to have recourse to the same words: "When the designated time had come, God sent forth his Son . . . " (Gal. 4:4); "God's love was revealed in our midst in this way: He sent his only Son to the world that we might have life through him" (1 John 4:9). Finally the book of Revelation, which provides a descriptive picture of the same reality of Jesus Christ, depicts the presence of the Son of man as a dynamic process. It does not present him as a king sitting on a throne or as an inert object of hieratic quality and cultic worship. Instead it shows him moving from heaven to earth: "See, he comes amid the clouds" (Rev. 1:7). The Spirit of the Church begs him to come, and three times he responds: "I am coming soon!" (Rev. 22:7, 12, 20). The notion of "coming" is so fundamental in the theology of John that it becomes at the very least a complementary aspect of God's being: God is he "who is and who was and who is to come" (Rev. 1:4, 8; 4:8). Thus in the New Testament the notion of "coming" takes on the universal scope that the notion of "being" has in philosophy. Just as being embraces the totality of the universe in the latter, so coming embraces the totality of the Christian mystery.

Most of the New Testament texts on the Gospel mission deal specifically with its origin or its objective. Everything done by Jesus goes back to his Father and is the result of a mission from him: "My doctrine is not my own; it comes from him who sent me" (John 7:16); "I have testimony greater than John's, namely, the works the Father has given me to accomplish. These very works which I perform testify on my behalf that the Father has sent me" (John 5:36). To whom is this mission directed? "I have come to call, not the self-righteous, but sinners" (Mark 9:13); "I came that they might have life, and have it to the full" (John 10:10); "I have come to the world as its light" (John 12:46).

In all the books of the New Testament we also find the notion that this mission is to be transmitted to his disciples and carried on by them. They too are sent, and the parallel between their mission and that of Jesus is brought out clearly. Jesus designated twelve "envoys" (Gr. *apostoloi)* and then told them what they were to do: "Go instead after the lost sheep of the house of Israel. As you go, make this announcement, 'The reign of God is at hand!' . . . " (Matt. 10:16–17); "Go, therefore, and make disciples of all the nations" (Matt. 28:19); "As the Father has sent me, so I send you" (John 20:21). The verbs "go," "send," and "come" describe the situation of the apostles even as they describe the situation of Jesus himself. And in the writings of Paul we see him in action as an envoy too.

The biblical texts, then, are familiar and indisputable.

But we must realize how a certain brand of theology has managed to de-emphasize them and almost empty them of content. First of all, it has reduced the Gospel mission to the world to an abstract schema. Being sent into the world is merely a way of describing the Incarnation, of alluding to the fact of becoming a human being and hence being born into the world. Jesus "came" into the world at the moment of his conception or birth. "Coming into the world" refers to the mystery of the Incarnation, and so classical theology can regard this "coming" just as Christology regards the salvific effect of the Incarnation, that is, as the set of preconditions that had to be met so that the mystery of redemption could be carried out. Jesus had to enter the world as a human being so that he could undergo his suffering, death, and resurrection as a human being and thereby become the fountainhead of salvation.

In such a schema the world is a purely abstract reality, simply the human nature necessary for the hypostatic union. The concrete world of human beings with their hopes and joys, their sufferings and sins, does not really enter the picture except as the intended beneficiary of the fruits of the redemption mystery. The mystery of redemption itself, however, is consummated outside of concrete human history; and the Gospel mission is merely an episode in the career of the hero of the whole drama. He had to come down to earth to play through a couple of acts, but otherwise the world and its population are mere spectators. In addition, the notions of "going" and "coming" can be applied in a derivative sense to the Parousia or to the coming of grace into the soul of the just person. It becomes a metaphorical mission, with no real movement in it.

Here we have a mystery of salvation that might have entranced someone like Dom Odo Casel. In this version we find all the elements of the gnostic mysteries that are celebrated in the myths of hellenism. And the only difference between the Christian drama and the gnostic mysteries would be that the former is true while the latter are not.

This viewpoint also deemphasizes the mission of the apostles. Their mission is simply to propose and proclaim the mystery of redemption to all peoples so that they can attain faith in it and thereby benefit from its fruits. As one missiologist put it, the Gospel mission comes down to planting the Church among all the peoples of the world so that the "means of salvation" can be made available to them in an organized way. Once again there is no sense of movement in this notion of the Gospel mission. It comes down to placing the means of salvation at the disposal of human beings.

Isn't this theology familiar to all of us, and shared by most of us to some extent? Yet the fact remains that it in no way explains the important role accorded to the Gospel mission in the New Testament and the stress placed on the themes of "coming," "going," and "sending."

I shall attempt to offer an alternative theology that does more justice to the biblical themes. Part One will deal with the essential aspects of the Gospel mission viewed intrinsically. Parts Two and Three will consider some important aspects of the Gospel mission insofar as it is bound up with human history.

THE GOSPEL MISSION IN ITSELF

4. Gospel Mission as Mission or Movement

The world of the New Testament is not some abstract entity. It is not "human nature" or humanity viewed as the "human species" or the earth viewed as a "planet" or "created matter." The world of the New Testament refers to concrete persons. When it tells us that Jesus came into the world, it means that "to his own he came, yet his own did not accept him" (John 1:11). "His own" are first and foremost the Jews: the people of Nazareth and Judea, the priests and the scribes, and many others. The reference is always to concrete human beings, for the Word came to talk to them. Each of them will be addressed and summoned, and the drama of salvation takes place in that process. It has nothing to do with any disembodied heaven so dear to the gnostic mysteries. Jesus Christ comes to establish an encounter with each individual person, and everything else revolves around that fact. Death and resurrection, the Father and the Spirit, the sacraments and Christian doctrines: All focus around the concrete act of encounter. In concrete form the encounters described in the Gospels are an analogy of what is going on in the depths of each human individual. Jesus came to address his message to Peter, John, and Andrew—to all the Peters, Johns, and Andrews of history. The words "coming," "going," and "sending" refer to this concrete act of summoning human beings in the midst of the human world.

The apostles are missionaries, people sent out. The title does not refer to actual journeys (which can be included under the heading of the Gospel mission), nor to some abstract application of the mystery of salvation. It applies to them because in their activities they serve the cause of Christ's summons to human beings. The mission of the apostles is not the repetition of Christ's mission, nor is it a numerically different one; it remains imbedded within Christ's own mission as his tool for appealing to human beings. The content, import, and underlying norm of the mission entrusted to Christians is the mission of Jesus himself. It ever remains an instrument of his mission, in the sense that it is a participation in that mission. It is the mission of Jesus Christ that makes apostolic acts what they are.

Salvation is accomplished at the moment when a person truly has an encounter with Jesus Christ. At that point Jesus tells the person that his faith has saved him. Salvation is not at all like the gnostic mysteries. It is an awakening of freedom and love by the Spirit and the summons of Jesus. But this act has a long history, embracing all the tragic and comic episodes of human history.

First of all, the envoy of Christ enters another's world, the world of an "other." Each person constitutes a universe. All people defend their own autonomy and react to external stimuli by rejecting, selecting, and transforming. What makes interpersonal communication difficult is precisely the fact that all individual persons judge perceived data by their own criteria and interpret everything in terms of their own world view, interests, and plans.

Missionaries do not belong to the universe of their

interlocutors. They are not foreseen or expected be-
forehand, and so they have no place in the latter's
scheme of things. Plans have already been made, and
missionaries are not covered by them. Time has already
been allotted, and there is none left for what the missionaries propose. That alone would explain why so
many doors are shut to them. And if it should happen
that provision has been made for the message of the
missionaries and that it does fit into the scheme of the
interlocutors, then there is reason to fear that the message of the missionaries is not the message of Jesus
Christ but rather a reflection of the interlocutors' own
world—in which case the latter see themselves reflected
in the object proposed and do not really have any objec-
tion to it.

Jesus, however, seeks to forestall the negative reaction, the closing up against his message. He tries to open
up a pathway so that he can get into the world of others,
unsettling them and awakening new aspirations. He
wants to awaken a new faith in life and its possibilities so
that he will eventually be recognized fully for who he is.
We see this process at work in the Gospel accounts and
also in our everyday life. That is why Jesus was sent: to
make his way into, and be accepted within, the inner
world of human beings and the outer world that they
project through their actions.

But this general tendency to close oneself off from
others is not the only obstacle. The spoken message of
Jesus Christ encounters a very specific form of resistance
known as sin; indeed his word brings sin to light. Why is
it that "his own did not accept him"? Here again the
Gospel narratives point to concrete cases as examples of
humanity as a whole. The resistance of the Pharisees and
scribes, of the Jews as a whole according to John, must be
extended to cover all humanity. The word of Jesus is a
kind of challenge that human beings are unwilling to

undertake. It awakens in them feelings of fright and anguish that lead to resistance and even total rejection. Jesus dies because he chooses not to respect the peace of mind of his interlocutors. The realization that they must change their way of life produces real panic in his audience. In our own personal way all of us live a life in which sin holds some place. To change means to destroy the harmonious balance already established and to launch out into the unknown, which is a frightening prospect.

Sin is so established and structured that it seriously infringes upon the liberty of human persons. There are strong social pressures in every society that tend to reinforce conformist behavior patterns. Interpersonal relationships, values, and the things that people regard as necessities are determined by social pressures affecting every member of a given society. Individuals are not free to decide most of their behavior patterns on their own initiative. Tradition and custom tend to determine social, economic, and sexual relationships. Even the forms of inequality, criminality, exploitation, and egotism are determined by social norms and customs (including the laws) and sanctioned by public opinion. If the socio-economic system is unjust, if the political system is unjust, if the relationship between social classes and the two sexes are marked by flagrant inequality, then one must be a real hero to stand up against the established system and pay the price for such a stand. A person who is lacking in charity can always say that everyone else acts the same way and that there is no point in making a spectacle of oneself.

Sin, then, is woven into the very texture of the world. Jesus found what we all find: that people's reactions are not based on personal options but on collective patterns. So it was with the scribes, the Pharisees, the Sadducees, the elders, and the Romans. Members of these groups accepted the group viewpoint and felt threatened by anyone or anything that placed their group in jeopardy. If people did want to make contact with Jesus, they would do what Nicodemus did. They would try to make contact with Jesus under the cover of night so that no one would know that they were undermining the rules of class solidarity. None of these people as individuals was responsible for Jesus' death; but as a group they were. The same thing holds true for almost all sins and crimes. The structure of social relationships means that no one is personally responsible because all are slaves of the system.

Thus Jesus Christ had to confront the structured forms of sin embodied in every group within his own people and in humanity as a whole. Being sent into the world meant being sent to confront the structures of sinfulness that enslave human beings. Further, human beings enjoy this bondage because it affords them refuge, security, and peace of mind. Nothing is more illusory than to think that human beings bemoan their enslavement and yearn for freedom. Authentic freedom, personal responsibility for one's own life, is the thing that human beings desire least.

"Sent to humankind" Jesus Christ attempts to penetrate the very core of the human personality. He wants to get beyond the fretwork of oppressive socio-cultural structures and to bring to life the more authentic human being that lies sleeping beneath the mask of the socialized human being. "Coming" to human beings does not simply mean traversing the face of the earth in the midst of human beings; it means looking for the authentic human being that is hidden away at the core of a person.

This mission of Jesus Christ goes on for each succeeding generation, occurring anew with the appearance of each new human individual. It is not confined to the past. Through the Spirit sent by him and through the mediation of his human apostles, Christ imperceptibly but really continues to perform the work that is described in an exemplary way by the Gospel accounts. The encounters mentioned in the New Testament are models and types that give us a rough picture of the spiritual encounters that have taken place every day since that time.

At times, and for certain purposes, Jesus uses the mediation of other human beings even though they are not the principal agents of the mission. The whole mission of the apostles has the same effect in view: to ensure that the word of Jesus Christ reaches concrete human beings in the inner depths of their authentic personalities. Each encounter is a dramatic adventure—some simple and straightforward, others very complicated.

This journey or movement toward human beings means that the Church is on the move, is a wayfaring Church. Here again, unfortunately, the notion can be emptied of all meaningful content so that it simply means that the Church manages to perdure through time: Like all human beings and human institutions, the Church goes through a host of experiences and adventures in history; it has many different experiences over the course of time as it operates through one culture after another, but it continues to do its work despite all the tribulations it faces. But this is a trivial conception, in which there is no trace of mystery. This is not the wayfaring journey and mission of Jesus Christ. Like Christ, the Church is called upon to make the journey from God to human beings, to tread the narrow and arduous roads that lead to human beings. Even when the physical distance is short, the journey itself may be long and difficult; but that is the journey which conditions the Church and defines its purpose. It cannot rest content within its own boundaries, lost in self-contemplation. It was established to go out towards human beings.

Insofar as the Church remains open and available to the service of Jesus Christ, it and its missionaries must remain flexible at all times. It comes from God and must go out to meet unknown human beings. It must assimilate the essential elements of God's message, divesting itself of past cultures that served other peoples and other circumstances and remaining independent of its own past so that it will not place unnecessary obstacles in the way of those who are not a part of that past.

The quality of "wayfaring" affects all the elements of the Church. Its message, for example, cannot be restricted to fixed formulas. It is really the word that Jesus addresses to human beings. We cannot hear or comprehend this word at the mysterious source where God pronounces it; nor can we listen to it at the point of arrival—i.e., in the minds and hearts of those who hear it. We grasp this word at an intermediary stage. What we hear now are the words that mediate between the message proclaimed by the risen Jesus and the message heard by human beings. If those intermediary words are to remain faithful to their source, they must be constantly analyzed, reformulated, and reinvented.

It is the Church that receives the words expressed by Jesus in human form as signs of God's word and message. It is the Church that tries to find the words capable of touching human hearts. In short, it is the Church that performs the constant task of mediation and translation. Its transmission of the message cannot be mere repetition of formulas, as it was in the case of the Jewish scribes. Mere formulas betray the word of God and do not reach the hearts of human beings. Real transmission of God's word entails a constant reinvention of the message so that it will accurately express the substance of the divine word to human beings. The message does not exist on its own as some fixed, prefabricated discourse, as some standing monument of the past, as a textbook for recitation. The message is a "wayfaring" one, calling for translation at every moment in time. It is what it is by virtue of the continuing effort of missionaries to transmit it in a vital way.

Experience tells us, however, that the Church is constantly tempted to stop this ongoing journey, to immobilize the message. The orthodoxy of its members must be preserved and defended, of course, but preoccupation with orthodoxy and heresy can kill the Gospel mission. If the message disappears under the formulas of councils and bishops, under the texts of creeds and condemnations, then there is a real danger that it will cease to be God's communication to human beings. Concern for orthodoxy may eliminate all concern for the Gospel mission. What use is it to pile up formulas that are perfectly orthodox if, in fact, they do not communicate the word of God to others? There is a real danger that the Church may talk so much to its own members that it will forget that its mission is to go out and speak to other human beings. It may end up talking and listening to itself, so that its mission and the Church itself disappear.

Missionaries do not really have any thinking of their own. Their thinking consists in listening to what comes from Jesus Christ and finding the words that can express that message in the language of other human beings. The language of God is a foreign language, which missionaries must translate into still another foreign language—that of human beings outside the Church. In the end the missionaries become merely channels of communication without any language of their own. To give the language of God a fixed form in ecclesiastical discourse is to give the wayfaring Church fixed form in established communities that are closed in upon themselves. The Gospel mission is suppressed, replaced by the work of administering to an established community. But the Acts of the Apostles shows us that the Spirit compelled the Church to move outside its own boundaries at the risk of persecution right from the start. The Spirit would not allow the Church to settle into established forms.

The priority of the Gospel mission means that it always remains more important than the work of administering already established groups, indeed that such groups cease to be legitimate when they tend to paralyze the mission effort. When the Church becomes an integral part of some given culture or society, then it becomes the instrument of human beings rather than the instrument of God.

Once a message is established in some fixed form, it is enunciated in terms of a given culture and it takes on the forms of that culture. The cultural system known as Christendom enunciated the Christian message in Greco-Roman terms, which were quite useful in proclaiming God's truth to Greeks and Romans. Reliance on those particular formulas caused missionaries to forget about carrying the divine message to other peoples. Or else it did something even worse. It prompted them to convey the message to other peoples in Greek and Roman terms, thus provoking a highly ambivalent reaction of rejection. To cite just one example, such has been the rejection of Christianity by broad sectors of modern Western culture.

What holds true for the message also holds true for the signs (i.e., the sacraments) and for all ecclesial institutions. It is the primacy of the Gospel mission that provides us with the governing criteria. Christians exist in order to speak to other people: That is the clear-cut conclusion to be derived from the words and parables and actions of Jesus.

Sometimes people appeal to the obligation to worship the Father in order to play down the Gospel mission to other human beings. They tell us that Christians have an obligation to seek out and converse with God. But the evangelists are very clear on this point. Jesus himself seeks out his Father and returns to him, but only after he has spoken to human beings. He was sent to human beings, and he cannot go back to the Father until he has carried out his mission. Therein lies the proper relationship between movement towards God on the one hand and movement towards human beings on the other. The mission starts out from God, but it cannot return to God until it has passed through the midst of human beings.

In this respect the Christian perspective is radically different from any religion. Religions are primarily concerned with God and only incidentally with human beings. Their concern for people serves only as propaganda on behalf of their God. But that is not true in the case of Christian mission. God does not need worship from anyone: God needs servants, ambassadors, people who will go out and talk to the people to whom God has not spoken. Ambassadors are not permitted to return before they have carried out the tasks assigned by those who have sent them. They have to speak their piece first. God is the ultimate origin and end of the Gospel mission, but God is not trying to compete for our love as we go about the mission task. Love of God and love of neighbor are one and the same: That is the first and basic principle of Christianity. Any real attempt to separate those two loves will destroy Christianity. The point deserves frequent repetition because we encounter repeated accusations of "horizontalism" and "modernism."

The first obligation of the missionary is the Gospel mission itself: "Preaching the Gospel is not the subject of a boast; I am under compulsion and have no choice. I am ruined if I do not preach it! If I do it willingly, I have my recompense; if unwillingly, I am nonetheless entrusted with a charge" (1 Cor. 9:16–17). The charge of the missionary is the charge of the Church itself, the Church who is the body of the missionary Christ.

The book of Revelation is the prophecy addressed to the churches toward the end of the first Christian generation. It is a summons to conversion motivated by the imminent coming of the Lord. But what reason lies behind the summons in this particular case? The letters addressed to the seven churches provide us with the answer to this question. These churches have lost their initial fervor and grown cold in the service of the Lord. They all need some reminder, at the very least, to bring them back to repentance: "You have turned aside from your early love. Keep firmly in mind the heights from which you have fallen" (Rev. 2:4); "I know your deeds; I know you are neither hot nor cold" (Rev. 3:15).

What "deeds" are in question here? The writer is referring to the deeds of the apostles, which should be the deeds of all Christians: bearing witness, prophesying, standing up in the great market centers to tell people about Christ, and so forth. These churches have stopped doing that. They have gone back to being a synagogue and have reintroduced all the notions and institutions of that Jewish center: laws, precepts, works of piety, and so forth. The Christian churches have taken on all the practices and forms that had come down through the Jewish and pagan peoples. The whole lifestyle of the Christian community has been changed, so that now the community is closed in upon itself. No longer is it concerned about the content of its laws and institutions.

Loyal members of an established religious community tend to forget the origin and reason behind their rites and institutions. They learn the catechism word for word but they are not concerned about the meaning of what it says. Why? Because such rites and institutions serve to define them as a community, to provide them with identification as individuals and members of a specific group. Thus the community lives its life in terms of itself alone in order to give its members feelings of security, worthiness, cohesiveness, and strength. That same temptation has threatened the Church of Christ from the very beginning. It has been tempted to function like every other religion concerned with ensuring its own effectiveness by concentrating on the needs of its own members.

Insofar as a Christian church gives in to that temptation, it has moved far away from its mission. The summons to conversion is the summons to return to the work of the Gospel mission. Throughout the history of the Church we note a never-ending appeal for reform. And while people may talk about individual reform, institutional reform, moral reform, and so forth, all of these take a back seat to the basic reform or conversion of the Church. First and foremost the Church must be converted, must turn its gaze to human beings and those outside its boundaries. It must go out to meet them, for everything else will follow naturally from this. All the forms of corruption to be found in Christians and their local churches come down to one basic fault: They have adapted too much to the customs and patterns of their milieu, allowing themselves to become an integral part of the surrounding culture.

But who are the "others" to whom we must turn? The Bible does not say explicitly. In any case they would not be the same people who stand in need of the word of Jesus Christ today. We cannot find them if we stay ensconced within our established communities. We must look outside those boundaries and go out in search of them. It is in this perspective that we should judge various initiatives undertaken by certain Christians in our own day. They are Christians undergoing conversion, Christians in search of the Gospel mission. Far from being oddities or extreme cases, they have come to realize the point the book of Revelation tried to make long ago, that is, that the Church has grown lukewarm and moved away from its primary works. They have set out as wayfarers on a search. And they are willing to become wayfarers in the strict and literal sense of the word should that become necessary.

Obviously this mission is much broader in scope than the visible boundaries of the Church. The Church extends far beyond its visible boundaries. It has been active and at work from the very beginning of the world, from the time of Abel, says Saint Augustine. Human beings have always gone out to meet other human beings with a message of salvation. Sometimes they may not even have known the name of the one who was sending them, or how to put into words the message that came through their gestures, actions, and silences. Yet God's word and message did resonate through them and people heard it. On the other hand we may find Catholics very devoted to the Church and happy with its presence who do not realize at all that it has a mission directed toward the "others."

5. Gospel Mission as Obedience

The Gospel mission makes no sense at all unless there is constant submission to the one who has sent out the missionary. The purpose of this mission is precisely to deliver or transmit a certain message. In this case, however, it is not merely a matter of receiving or accepting some message that has been put in objective form. A typical human message can be set down in writing and memorized when it is delivered by a human messenger. But in our case the message is the mission of Jesus Christ himself. It entails calling attention to the presence of Jesus Christ and fleshing out the signs that will render that presence vital and operative.

The worst temptation of all is the temptation to condense the object of the Gospel mission into some cold and lifeless text. The old catechisms used to pose this question: What are the truths we must believe in order to be saved? As if God really demanded that we learn certain formulas by rote memory! As if it were all a matter of learning certain words by an act of will! As if a bride needed to be taught her bridegroom's declarations of love! As if children had to be taught the expressions of affection voiced by their mother! And yet the fact remains that Christianity is transformed into a compendium of dogmas, ritual gestures, and customs. In that case we are clearly no longer dealing with a mission that involves speaking to the hearts of human beings, particularly to those others who are outside the Church. Instead we are simply left with the task of integrating a new generation into the established socio-cultural system. But that represents a supreme act of disobedience, for Jesus did not establish a new synagogue. His purpose was to launch God's mission, or to launch it anew; to address himself to human beings through the mediation of human beings.

Insofar as the words took on formal shape and were transformed into credal codes, the ministers of those codes ceased to be submissive to God. Those formal codes do not derive from God but from the human authorities who formulated them. Jesus reminded the people of his own time and place that their codes came from Moses, not from God. There is a big difference! Now it is true that the institution of the code is attributed to God himself, but we must be careful how we interpret that. Such a code can appeal to the authority of God to the extent that it effectively serves to advance the work of God's mission. But the authority of God as guarantee fades away to the extent that the code departs from the mission assigned by God.

It is expected of missionaries that they will keep listening to and assimilating what Jesus Christ is saying to human beings, that they will continue to pay heed to the divine word that seeks to touch the inner depths of human beings and bring to life the new person. That divine word does not find expression as such in dry discourses. It finds expression in real life, in human gestures that can somehow be more than human—or fully human, if you prefer. Learning the divine message is not a one-shot process. We must keep listening and learning in each particular situation. Christ does not speak to each individual in exactly the same way. The pace of conversation, the points stressed, and the arrangement of content differ from one individual to the next.

The Spirit was given to help us with our obedience. As Jesus tells his disciples after the Last Supper, the mission of the Spirit is to be of service to the apostles, to help them comprehend the import of Jesus' own words. But longstanding habit and routine tend to undermine our belief in and our need for the Spirit. If it is simply a matter of handling the administrative affairs of ecclesiastical society, then the intervention of the Spirit is scarcely necessary. We really do not need the Spirit to make up a catechism, to collect the viewpoints of theologians and publish theology manuals, to compose pious discourses and proclaim the grandeur of the Creator. With the aid of a few good approaches and techniques and with the support of a good training program everything will run quite smoothly. Sound competence, once acquired, will be useful and valuable always; so we can plan for the future and assign each individual a role in the overall process.

But none of this will function if our real task is to say to the non-Christians what Jesus himself wants to say to them, if our human gestures and actions are supposed to transmit the message that Jesus Christ wants to communicate. It won't be accomplished by a training program, a good technique, a smooth approach, or merely acquired skill. Something more complicated is involved, and it can be summed up in a simple phrase: submission to the Spirit.

Submission to the Spirit and a real living out of that obedience do not come to us easily or spontaneously. Indeed they are rare phenomena in the Church. The predominant attitude tends to be one of self-sufficiency, and it is particularly evident among the clergy and our religious congregations. Perhaps I should say that the attitude used to be fairly common, for more recent events have compelled us to qualify our statement.

This attitude of self-sufficiency stems from many varied initiatives and works to which we can point. It is a holdover from the days of cultural Christendom when church propaganda convinced people that the Church had an answer for every problem. The Church and its clergy were inclined to get involved in everything, to establish projects of every sort. But the experience of history does not seem to prove that clergy and religious are more capable of solving problems than other people are. The point has not been verified anywhere in the world. And even if one were to accept the assumption that the projects headed by the clergy have somehow been more efficient and effective than those undertaken by lay people, the very monopoly exercised by the clergy tends to devaluate the laity and close off their access to positions of adult responsibility. And finally we must realize that Jesus Christ himself did not step into the picture to solve any problem facing his contemporaries. It is clear that he did not possess the capacity to solve their problems, and that he knew he did not. Jesus "emptied himself," becoming a plain and simple human being without any special expertise. He made no claims to any qualities that would win human power or glory, that would represent a high degree of human knowledge or know-how. Why should we or the Church try to be stronger than our Master?

The many works undertaken by the Church tend to instill a feeling of tranquillity and self-sufficiency, for they are in no need of inspiration from the Spirit. Their results are inscribed in the socio-economic situation. One does not have to rely on the Spirit to envision and build a school, a cooperative, or a hospital. One need only read and interpret the material situation of the country to arrive at such a project. The problem is: Can we be sure that these projects represent God's loving word to the forlorn, the sinful, and the neglected human beings of the world? Historians tell us that the Curé of Ars was always asking himself whether he was doing right or wrong, whether he was on the right track or not. He certainly was not concerned about purely moralistic considerations, about whether or not he was sinning against the commandments of God and the Church. His problem was trying to find out whether he was wasting his time by doing merely human things or whether he was in fact obeying the inspiration of the Spirit. It is not an easy question to answer. Indeed it is much easier to rest content with an encouraging word or a pat on the back from one's pastor or bishop. And since they tend to approve and bless everything, their approbation means very little. For that matter, they cannot be too sure about their own work. From what do they derive their certainty and security? There is no great problem in organizing and running things within the framework of an established society. But doesn't the Gospel mission go above and beyond the good features of a well-organized society? Jesus could have organized a synagogue, a school, a dispensary. But he did not. Why? What is the secret of his mission?

Living in total obedience to the Spirit does not mean trying to get an authoritative seal of approval stamped on the things that we would be doing anyway because they suited our aspirations and perhaps even our convenience. That kind of obedience is a virtue only for functionaries and mercenaries. Obedience to the Spirit means that we constantly refer and relate our initiatives to the Spirit.

And it is here that the problem arises. How can we come to know and correctly interpret the inspiration of the Spirit? It certainly cannot be framed in any fixed or established code. The inspiration of the Spirit is personal in nature, or directed to a specific group. It evolves and changes, and we can never be sure of having the Spirit in our grasp. As Jesus tells us, the Spirit is like the wind that blows where it wills. We must also rule out the idea that there are certain persons entrusted with the task of receiving and communicating the inspirations of the Spirit. Such delegation does not exist. The authority of the ecclesiastical hierarchy is in the prudential order; it is designed to help maintain order within the ecclesial community. A member of the hierarchy can never know whether a person should or should not do a certain thing.

At this point the moralists of old appealed to the sovereignty of conscience. But in our case individual conscience is even less in a position to be able to say whether it has encountered the inspiration of the Spirit. The Spirit does not intervene by way of personal conscience and its experience. Missionaries will not discover the inspiration of the Spirit or the mission they are supposed to carry out by reflecting on their own conscience.

What, then, is the right approach? The classic answer is that we must look to *the signs of the times.* Much could be said about this notion, and it deserves to be examined in all of its aspects. But for our purposes here, we need only consider certain basic aspects that are related to our theme.

The signs of the times are not imbedded in the purely material conditions of the world or in its purely material evolution. The material aspect is clearly of indirect relevance because it is the basis of all change. But it does not concern us directly here because the Gospel mission does not grant us any special ability to comprehend the biological, sociological, or anthropological laws governing the world's evolution. Christians are no more capable in this respect than others. They have not been given any new tool that enables them to better understand the objective evolution of the world. The Spirit is not manifested through scientific discoveries, new technologies, or socio-economic development. If we want to interpret the signs of the times, we do not really make any progress by devoting our attention to the physical, technological, or economic evolution of the world. This material time is of no direct significance.

What, then do the times point out to us? What does signify the Spirit? Before we try to answer those questions, let us first ask another preliminary question. What exactly do the signs signify? What sort of signal are we looking for? We are looking for signs that have to do with the Gospel mission, for signs that show us how we are to communicate God's love to human beings of the present day. More specifically we are looking for signs that will show us how to communicate that love to a specific individual, a specific group, a specific nation. We are scanning the external world to find something that will help us to see what road our mission should take. Obviously our answer will not be found in nature, in inert things, in manufactured products, in industry, or in science. In terms of our framework here, the characteristic note of present-day reality that will serve as our sign is not the atomic bomb, or television, or antibiotics, or moon flights. The sign-bearing happenings will be found in certain actions of other people, of other human beings. Scrutinizing the signs of the times means looking closely at the actions of *others*. The Spirit does not speak to us through conscience or personal reflection; the Spirit speaks to us through *other people*. The Spirit brings us in contact with others so that their way of acting may enlighten us. The sin of self-sufficiency prompts the Christian and every human individual to gain knowledge solely through the self. Christ bids us to look at others and gain enlightenment from them.

If we stay closed up in ourselves, we will not find out anything. Instead we must keep our eye on what is happening in the world outside us. It is not a question of statistics. The behavior of the average person or of the majority reveals nothing but the mediocrity of human beings and reflects nothing but the impact of established structures and social conformity. But in the midst of the crowd there are charismatic human beings endowed with the gifts of the Spirit; there are people who can show us how we might manifest God's love for human beings. It is not necessary that they themselves be aware of the sign value of their actions. Certain actions will often have import for some people but not for others. That does not matter. It will also happen that the sign-bearing persons and actions will not be associated with the Church in a visible way. They need not be Christian in that sense.

On this point the Gospel writers are very instructive. What sort of signs does Jesus point to? What sort of people does he call attention to? Among others, the Gospel narratives call our attention to a Samaritan, a Roman centurion, a Syro-Phoenician, pagan woman, a prostitute, a blind man, and a publican. How many scribes or priests or pious Israelites were singled out by Jesus as people with real sign value? None. Perhaps we must take the same approach today. Perhaps we must look for signs of the times among the publicans and sinners and atheists of our day. Perhaps our lack of inspiration stems from our unwillingness to look for the signs of the times in the world outside us. Perhaps it is there that we shall find the gestures and deeds that manifest God's love, that "evangelize"! If we want to translate that message into human terms comprehensible to our contemporaries, must we not look to the poor Samaritans and sinners of our own day?

To be sure, Jesus had no intention of saying that the

Samaritan religion was better than the Jewish religion, or that sin was better than virtue. He was simply trying to make the point that the Spirit is free to make use of Samaritans and sinners. The example of Jesus himself leads us to believe that God does have a predilection for such people. On our own, of course, we would not be inclined to look in their direction for inspiration. But shouldn't the Spirit's approach be given due consideration in our appraisal of the matter?

In any case interpretation of the signs of the times could never be a complicated task left to experts. It does not require special offices, commissions, and administrative organs. Such signs are within the scope of every human being, even the most untutored. That is why God selected the simplest people to show missionaries what road they should take. It is up to us to understand and appreciate what these despised outcasts are saying, to grasp the lessons they are trying to teach us, to follow in their footsteps so that we may be able to carry out our task.

If we travel by way of the established ecclesial communities, we will always be inclined to think that the essential work of the Gospel mission is to repeat the traditional gestures: to preach dogmas, administer the sacraments, mouth moral precepts, and convene meetings. All that may be useful, and it is under certain circumstances, but it is not essential. The essential thing is what Jesus said to the pagans, to those outside the established system. He tried to make them aware of a new life and to win their conversion to it. This should suggest that we cannot be content with the convenience of long-established routines.

Another indicator of ambivalence on the part of missionaries is the multiplicity of the initiatives and tasks they undertake. This can be a sign of abundant charismatic gifts, but it can also be a sign of a compulsion to "do something" in the absence of charisms. One must know how to wait. This capability has been described in terms of the "contemplative life," which is a sadly inadequate term and heavily tinged by Greek philosophic thought. We must know how to wait until the signals are sufficiently clear, until the right moment is at hand. There is no sense doing the same thing twice when once would be enough. There is no sense needlessly prolonging the life of structures and institutions which have outlived their purpose. We must be wise enough to wait in silence so that we are not simply carried along by the rhythm of our activities and fall prey to inertia. The tendency to overindulge in activities and an inability to wait in prayerful silence for the Spirit's manifestation are two typical forms of disobedience to the Spirit.

When the time for action comes, however, this same obedience to the Spirit calls for what St. Paul terms apostolic "boldness." If the action is truly inspired by the Spirit, then it is not the limited activity of a limited person. Truly missionary activity elevates the missionary to the level of authentic universality, and here I am not talking about a static universality bound up with some social role or function. In the latter instance those exercising a social role enter into the overall flow of a given society and become participants in that society as a totality. They feel that they are participants in a project that is broader than that of just an individual, a project that is part of a whole. That is the common image of universality. But the fact is that no action of role framed in those terms (e.g., a laborer, a doctor, a teacher, a bishop) really gets beyond the limited boundaries of a specific society. It is not an action over and above society; it is an action within society. It does not transform society, it serves to integrate it.

Authentic missionaries tend to give rise to something new. However modest and lowly it may be, the missionaries know that if it really is inspired by the Holy Spirit it is the seed that will grow into a new tree. Their activity takes on universal dimensions, going above and beyond a given society in order to change it. On the one hand they feel lost, without prestige or function or honor or official recognition from society. On the other hand they feel confident that their lowly and obscure activity is the most universal activity possible, that in the long run it will have the greatest effect and influence on the destiny of humanity. Its seeming lowliness in the present is the precondition for its future fruitfulness.

Missionaries can always glimpse this universality in the modest objects of their activity or in the concrete people affected by it. The universality does not lie in the importance of the people among whom they are living and with whom they are sharing the message they have received. The people may well be insignificant in the eyes of the established society. The universality stems from a dynamic principle, from the certainty that a new world is in the making among seemingly insignificant people, for there is where the Spirit has chosen to enter the world. The Gospel mission is never abstract, nor is it ever addressed to some abstract human category. It always revolves around concrete people, proceeding from there to renew and revitalize society and the world as a whole. The whole history of the Church confirms this law of universality—not just the history of the visible Church but also the history of charity and salvation at work among human beings everywhere in the world. Most of this history remains hidden from view, but what does come to light demonstrates the consistency and persistency of the Spirit's way of working.

Hence the boldness of the apostles. They do not act in their own name. Instead their work is the expression of a higher activity. In all their actions the missionaries commit Christ himself to the project. There is no distinction between the actions in general of Christians and their actions as Christians as such. By their very vocation Christians are missionaries, and all their actions in life commit Christ and the Church to the world. There is no place for purely personal options that have to do with our own welfare. There is only one option, the option of Christ himself, when we are trying to save our neighbor. We can choose this option or reject it, but there is no third alternative. We may unwittingly deceive ourselves or make a mistake, but our only choice in the name of Jesus is obedience. Only that gives value to our deeds.

After pondering the above considerations, some readers might well feel concern about age-old ecclesiastical institutions. How are we to save them? How can we justify them within the theological framework just outlined? But the task of theology is not to save the things of old by offering more solid, up-to-date arguments in their support. What we need is a well-rounded, overall vision so that we can fit the things of old into their proper place. The fact is that they know very well how to fend for themselves, for they can always rely on the weighty influence of routine and tradition.

The real problem lies elsewhere. How can we rediscover something of the "folly" of Jesus Christ—to use Paul's term—in the midst of so much ecclesiastical wisdom? There seems to be no absence of wisdom, but what has happened to the "folly"? What we are really looking for is that seed of folly that will keep Christianity from becoming too wise, too well integrated, too much like any other religion or philosophy in this world.

The concept of the Gospel mission lies at the heart of the great theological problems of our day. Since Christianity is a mission, it is not some parallel "world" or "life." It is the movement of God toward us and us toward God. It is not some part of humanity but humanity in its totality. We encounter Jesus Christ in the middle of this movement. Or, to put it more accurately, he *is* this movement. He is the one who "comes to" human beings, the word resounding in their ears. He is the one who stands at the door and knocks. His mission is one of thoroughgoing obedience to the Father, and that of others is merely a prolongation of the same obedience.

So now we must move on to consider the content and object of the Gospel mission. What is communicated in this mission? For what was Jesus sent? The answer is: salvation. But what does "salvation" mean? That is what we shall consider in the next section. Then we shall go on to consider the way in which the Gospel mission is carried out, the way in which it brings salvation. We shall see that it does this by way of service, that strength in weakness is its distinctive resource. Then, finally, we shall stress the public character of the Gospel mission, which is directed simultaneously to the individual person and to society as a whole.

6. Gospel Mission as Salvation

First of all salvation is something new, a happening, a new reality in the world. What exactly is this reality? In other words, what is the content of salvation? Salvation is also an action. What sort of action is it? Finally salvation is something lived by the person who is saved. What does it really mean to be saved? These three points will be considered separately in this section.

The objective of salvation. Countless theological debates have only served to upset people's thinking and to obscure the point that the Bible proclaims from first page to last, i.e., that everything God does in this world—past, present, and future—is done with human beings as its object. The first biblical account culminates in the creation of the human being, the center of nature; and the last page of the Bible presents a vision of the saved person as the center of all history. The mission of Jesus Christ had no other purpose. He became man so that all might truly be human in him. Salvation is intended to make sure that human beings will truly be human in the fullest sense of the word. We had lost our humanity, had somehow ceased to be truly human. The evil lay in us, and salvation would represent our liberation from all that prevented us from being truly human. And what is it that prevents us from being truly human? It is we ourselves.

The problem confronting Christianity can be defined in terms of evil, which is not something external to us. If that were the case, we would only have to remove the evil to bring freedom and salvation to humankind. To be sure, there is also evil in exterior things, but these things originate in us. Salvation must get to the root of the evil, which lies in us. We are the source of all the forms of domination we find, of all the structures tainted with evil. What we call sin is really an evil whose roots lie in us. If human beings are to be truly human, then we must be liberated from the evil that lies within us.

Socio-economic structures of domination and exploitation are not ultimately rooted in external juridical forms that we might reform or replace; nor are they rooted in the perverse thinking of one particular human group. They are rooted in all human beings, for we all have a tendency to create new structures of domination and oppression that embody our yearnings for special privilege and pride of place. And these structures are maintained thanks to the collaboration or silence or cowardice of countless human beings. Evil is rooted in the abuse of human will power whereby some latch hold of an opportunity to dominate others, and in the cowardice of those who are willing to put up with all forms of injustice.

So it is not easy to be a human being. It is hard to continue being honest, upright, truthful, and just. As we know, only saints and heroes can manage it. The average human being soon loses the high-minded ideals of adolescence, if we ever entertained them at all. We soon learn that the honest person lives a fairly wretched life, that we cannot "make it" that way. Millions of petty dishonesties go into the making of an unjust society where we are gradually destroyed by the structures that our own cowardice maintains.

The object of the Gospel message is to teach us how to be authentic human beings. The objective of salvation is to make sure that we will be human beings in the fullest sense of the word. And that will entail a long process of winning mastery by ourselves and for ourselves.

The human being is an eschatological reality. In fact, when all is said and done, we are the primary and perhaps only eschatological reality. The world, too, is an eschatological reality, but it is really a prolongation of us and does not lie outside us. We cannot define the human person in terms of any static philosophy, much less in terms of any human science based on observation. For we are, first and foremost, something that is not as yet. Our authentic reality is precisely that which we do not yet do. Each of us need only look at ourself and ask if our life is truly worthy of a human being. We would do well to ponder the criticisms and denunciations of the great secular prophets of the past hundred years (Nietzsche, Marx, Freud, and others). It soon becomes evident that we find our full humanity at the end of a long process, and this process is what we call salvation.

Christianity maintains simultaneously both that the roots of evil lie in us and that this evil can be combatted; both that salvation is necessary and that it is possible. Christianity holds that we are flexible and changeable, not fixed in our plight. Thus Christianity rejects the dualistic extremes that have often dominated human thought. Human wisdom has often posed the problem in terms of two mutually exclusive alternatives: Either we deny the existence of evil or we declare it incurable. Christianity affirms both the existence of evil and the possibility of salvation, thereby transforming history into the drama of our salvation.

This leads us to conclude that any attempt to separate evangelization and humanization would destroy the very core of Christianity. Preaching the Gospel is the mission of Jesus Christ, but the Gospel is not just a spoken word; it is an efficacious word that brings about what it proclaims. The purpose and end result of evangelization is our salvation. It saves us from evil, from the cowardice that prevents us from being truly human. It sets us on the road to being revitalized. Is that not a process of humanization?

In some strands of current theological thinking this equivalence does not show up clearly because the notion of communion with God and participation in the divine life is isolated from the notion of humanization. But it is difficult to conceive of any participation in the divine life that would not entail living human life to the full. Being a child of God cannot possibly be something different from being a full and complete human being. Elevation to the supernatural order does not alter the human essence. Instead it raises it to its full measure, which goes above and beyond the limits of nature, as the theology of an older day would put it. But elevation to the supernatural order cannot create some realm of existence that is separate or distinct from our life as human beings. To be a child of God is to be a human being. Living the life of a human being, one is raised to a sharing in the life of God, which means that the process of humanization is carried through to its full measure of perfection.

Most of the difficulties and objections posed to this theological view stem from the anthropology that underlies the prevailing ideologies of the present day. The most pervasive and forceful of these ideologies is the positivism of the Western world, for it has served as the inspiration for neocapitalism, nationalism, and Marxism. The feature shared by all these ideologies is their objectification of the human being. They look from the outside, viewing the person as a focal point of varied needs, aspirations, relations, and satisfactions. Viewed in this light, the person is an object of manipulation by various social factors (political authority, economic power, group pressure, and so forth). Such processes as development and humanization are processes worked to effect a transformation from the outside. To humanize means simply to set in motion certain objective forces of whatever sort in order to alter the internal or external forces that work on the person. It is simply a matter of engineering. The aim is to transform human beings without they themselves having to change in any way. Since the person is viewed as the product of various structures, all we have to do is change those structures. Or, if we go beyond that, we assume people will change themselves once the external structures are altered.

There is no doubt that we must change external structures in order to save the human person, but the fact remains that such structural changes will always be ambivalent. The tactics and techniques used to change people are manipulated by people, and so they do not automatically effect the liberation of human beings. They will effect this liberation only when they are in the hands of human beings who have saved themselves from evil. In the hands of sinful human beings, however, the techniques of structural change will only produce new structures of domination and oppression. Our present-day experience has taught us that the human sciences, the techniques of development, and the capacity to change structures are capable of engineering new and unheard of forms of oppression. Work on structures is ultimately worth only as much as the human beings who do that work, for the end result is the product of all the decisions that have gone into the effort.

We are not just a complex of varied functions. First and foremost we are beings personally responsible for our decisions and deeds, even though our responsibility may be infinitesimal in a given instance. It is that particle of responsibility, however miniscule it may be, that makes us human beings. Without that particle of personal freedom and responsibility we are nothing but a complex machine. It is that particle of personal freedom that is the source of all human reform and transformation. There is no reform program or salvation plan that does not emanate from human beings. There is no absolute point of reference, no objective or neutral scientific bureau of human salvation. Every plan emanates from human beings, who incorporate into it their authentic freedom or their corruption.

Saving the human person means relying on an appeal to the freedom and sense of responsibility found in the heart of everyone. It means counting on the convergence of countless individual liberties, for every bit of good in the world derives from that source. The act which flows from freedom is love, and all love presupposes human beings who have rediscovered something of their freedom. Freedom and love are the two basic concepts of Christian anthropology, the two basic themes of eschatology, the two basic fruits of Christ's salvific work. Salvation consists in reconstructing freedom and love in human beings and, in the last analysis, this cannot be done from the outside. We may alter every existing structure, but in the last analysis we ourselves must liberate our own freedom and make use of it; we must dare to love, and no one can do that for another.

All the structures of human life proceed from us. If we are saved, those structures will be saved. But the root of salvation lies in the salvation of human beings as the active subjects who fashion themselves, who exercise freedom and love, which are the ultimate wellsprings of everything human after God the creator.

What are we to be saved from? We must be saved from

the powers that oppress and enslave us, to use the words of Scripture. In the concrete these powers are the personal and societal structures of every culture and civilization in which human beings live; this would include ideological structures, socio-economic structures, patterns of thought and social behavior, and so forth. These structures help us to live, but they ever remain ambivalent, because we invest and incorporate both our humaneness and our lack of humanity into them. They always represent a precarious balance between justice and injustice, between projects designed to establish greater equity and maneuvers designed to take personal advantage of a situation. It is not a matter of wiping out these structures and their potential, but rather of transforming them so that they can fulfill their legitimate role and express human freedom and love between human beings.

For this very reason the salvific plan and the salvific forces embodied in Jesus Christ have been the wellspring of many revolutions in the past—revolutions in the life of the spirit and in economic life. But all revolutions give rise to new forms of domination insofar as they are effected by corrupt human beings who are not fully free.

On a deeper level than any revolution we discover the true leaven of Christianity. It entails a process of resurrection within people themselves, a process of justification in the root sense of that word. We must be made just, but only we can accomplish this. This is where the notion of humanization enters in its most radical sense. It does not mean giving salvation to people, for that is impossible in any case. You cannot give freedom to a human being. Freedom and love proceed from human beings themselves. Thus Jesus Christ does not work *on* the structure of humanity. Instead he works *at the source* from which freedom and love spring.

Freedom and love are not won once and for all. Who

can say that they are securely ensconced in freedom and love, that they are in no danger of backsliding? Who can claim any absolute guarantee? We live, or are called to live, a dynamic ongoing process in which our freedom and love are constantly refashioned anew. There is no way of evading the task.

So we can say that the salvation of Jesus Christ is mystical and political at the same time. It is political because we live enslaved to oppressive structures from which we must free ourselves in order to establish justice. It is mystical because this effort would turn into another form of oppression if it were not motivated by, and suffused with, human freedom and love.

Never before in history have we seen so many plans for liberation as are evident in our day. Yet this century has produced the most perfectly worked out systems of domination in human history—all promising salvation. The resources of science and technology can serve any purpose. A program of reform will engender freedom if it is supported by thousands of individual free wills. But no structure can give rise to freedom if it is not constantly watched and maintained and altered by a host of free human beings who are determined to accept their fellow human beings.

It is true that the ideologies of the present day profess great respect for individual human beings and solicit their freely proffered collaboration. They all posit the person as the starting point and end point of their ideological structure. But somehow the individual human being is left out when it comes to concrete action and implementation. At that point all initiative and control ends up in the hands of some elite group, whose members claim to know exactly what is needed. They alone seem to be capable of establishing authentic justice because they alone, it seems, know how to administer and manage matters. They begin by prescinding from

Christianity in their attempt to effect salvation. They end up by prescinding from people themselves and claiming that true human freedom comes down to accepting and acclaiming the program they propose.

Authentic salvation, however, is resurrection to freedom and love. But how can we act in such a way that this will be accomplished. Won't any action designed to produce freedom prove to be self-contradictory?

Salvation in action. Who can set freedom in motion from within and stir love into action at its source? Who can change us in such a way that we ourselves are truly the author of the change, that it is not just the reflex response to stimuli imposed from the outside? Who can liberate us from the sin of not wanting or willing to be free—for whatever reasons—and from the inability to love?

The Bible tells us that this is the work of Jesus Christ. How does he do it? He does it through the spoken word, that is to say, through a personal encounter with human beings. As a human being he speaks to another human being, overcoming the barriers that have been set up. According to Scripture, he is a human being whose spoken word has the value and force of God's word. What stirs and moves us in the depths of our being is the summons of Jesus Christ. Raised from the dead, he is present and alive and at work as the one who has been sent to us.

The effect of Jesus' word is to awaken freedom and love, as we can tell from reading about his meetings with human beings. The Gospels make clear the power of his word and his presence in concrete historical terms, and the very same process is continually going on in human beings and their lives ever since. Jesus' meeting with them embodies the active power of resurrection whereby the dead are transformed into the living, the sinful into the just.

The human followers of Jesus Christ, the apostles,

have a place in his mission, in his encounter with human beings. Their mission is a part of this encounter. The purpose of all their actions is to make known the person of Jesus Christ, to depict him not as some absent figure but as a living, active presence. Their activity is the visible sign of the ongoing activity of Jesus Christ.

When I use the term "word" or "spoken word" here, I am using it in its biblical sense. In the Bible the term "word" connotes an active force that expresses love and is capable of awakening another love in response, that expresses freedom and is capable of awakening a taste for freedom in response. Its power can be described as reciprocity, the reciprocity of the creator who awakened his creature and stimulated the first stirrings of love within him.

Our ability to comprehend the mystery of Jesus Christ is complicated by the fact that we are still tangled up in mental constructs that hearken back to the times of mythology. The theology of antiquity and the Middle Ages misused images derived from various mythologies. For example, it took the credal formula that "Christ died for our sins" and interpreted it in mythological categories, picturing it in terms of ancient myths of sacrifice. In these, sacrifices were thought to have almost magical power to affect supernatural forces. A sacrifice was efficacious in itself. It is very strange that this notion was applied to Christ, for the whole New Testament rules out such an idea. It is not the moment of Jesus' death as such, nor the act of dying as such, that is salvific. The Savior is not the dead Christ but the risen Christ who brings salvation in spite of death; for God has given him life and the power to save.

What about the usual picture of the efficacious nature of his death, in which he is punished for our sins so that human beings may attain salvation? This rationalization is frankly horrible. The image of Jesus' meritorious death as "satisfaction," which is based on the feudal notion of satisfaction for injuries, is wholly irrational. The whole schema of merit is sheer moralism. It makes salvation something that descends on us, and it is based on an abstract principle that is a vestige of paganism. The Gospels clearly affirm that it is the risen Christ who is the Savior, and that he comes into the midst of human beings in order to speak to them and act in them. That is what salvation is. Jesus' death is efficacious because it is the gateway to resurrection. Resurrection is not efficacious insofar as it is a fact or a status. The one who saves is the Christ who lived on earth, bore witness, inaugurated his mission, and died for that reason. But God resurrected him, thus offering his own witness and showing that life is stronger than human hatred, the gift of righteousness stronger than the resistance of sin. The mission of the Church is faithfully to interpret and serve that mission, not as a material instrument of some magical power but as a group of persons serving as signs of a summons to freedom and love.

The statement that "Jesus died for our sins" is a succinct summary of a long process. Jesus died because he stood up against sin but human beings were reluctant to follow him. His death was the outcome of his struggle against sin, his faithful witness to the very end. His martyrdom was a summons, clearing the road for us and combatting fear, resignation, and ambivalence. It was an act of confidence in truth and love. At the same time, however, it seemed to give the lie to everything that Jesus had said; the resurrection thus provided confirmation of his message.

Jesus' death was an act of confidence in his Father, in the Father who had entrusted him with a mission. The Father could not abandon him, and his response to Jesus' death was to give him life. The Father overcame death, and so the sign of failure was transformed into a sign of victory through the resurrection. Raised from the dead, Jesus became the Savior. His testimony was confirmed by his death and resurrection. As the witness of a living man who is the son of God, it represents the great encounter with the Other and serves as a stimulus for all of us.

Encounter with Jesus is not a purely mythical phenomenon, an exceptional experience, or an abstract concept. He makes his presence felt regularly in and through our encounters with a concrete human being whose words, freedom, and love represent a revelation and a summons. Thus human beings become part of the saving action of Jesus Christ, or instruments of it at the very least. That in fact is how the Gospel message is transmitted—from one human being to another. Contact with a certain human being is the sign of one's encounter with Jesus Christ, the starting point for conversion. No one can be an authentic Christian without going through such an experience. Mystical phenomena are exceptional and unnecessary. They are always a bit off the track and reflect a specific culture. Contact with concrete Christians is the ordinary way in which human beings encounter Jesus Christ.

The point already mentioned also applies here. The persons who serve as signs of Jesus Christ, as signs of charity and freedom, need not be Christians or Catholics. Such people have existed from the beginning of the world. They may be authentic signals of his presence even though they fail to acknowledge him after hearing his word. Indeed the end result of conversion, the awakening of freedom and love, can be effected without invoking the name of the one who is the author of this salvation. The important thing is that Christ is actually at work, whether his name is invoked or not. Pagans can teach us lessons about true knowledge of Christ and fidelity to his mission, whereas professed Christians can fail to be instruments of his mission. The Gospels clearly foresaw these possibilities.

Salvation in the saved person. We can also look at salvation in terms of its end result. We can consider the real-life situations of the saved persons. We can look at the people who are in the process of regaining their full humanity, thanks to salvation. Human beings are truly human insofar as they manage to win their humanity, overcoming themselves in the first place and then overcoming the structures that restrict their humanity.

Salvation exists in those human beings who have awakened to authentic freedom and discovered charity. It must be pointed out that this sign is not peculiar to Christians, that others also bear witness to it. The Gospel accounts confirm this fact, for the great example of charity is the Samaritan. Jesus makes clear to us that our models are to be found, not among his disciples, but among outsiders. The voice of Jesus resounds beyond the borders of official ecclesiastical institutions.

The initial phase of salvation is faith. Faith is our response to our encounter with Jesus. It is an awakening to a new personhood, a discovery of something entirely new, thanks to an encounter with Jesus Christ. The rest of the Christian way of life follows from that awakening to freedom and love. Faith, then, is the overall act of opening up and becoming receptive to the presence of Jesus Christ. Professions of faith, creeds, and dogmas are merely an explicitation of this initial faith in response to needs that are not properly those of faith itself (e.g., the need for group communication, mutual recognition, and cohesiveness).

Some schools of present-day theological thought completely separate the act of faith from human life, as if the former were an escape hatch into another world completely isolated from this one. But in fact faith in Jesus Christ represents the liberation and fullness of the timid, insecure, and ambivalent faith that lies buried in the heart of every human being. One cannot live at all without some initial spark of faith. One must believe a little in life and love, in the possibility of doing something sound and good in life. Faith in Jesus Christ follows along this line. To believe in him is to recognize in him the truth about ourselves, a truth that had not been perceived or hoped for in any strict sense before. Through faith in him, which presupposes some prior faith in life, we come to see the right road and to glimpse light and life.

This Christian faith is also the salvation of initial human faith, revealing its depths and giving it confirmation. It helps to solidify the truth that we all hear resounding within ourselves in some vague or obscure way. Coming from the outside, the word of Christ sheds light on the confused chorus of voices within the individual and confirms the primacy of freedom and love in the face of adverse experiences and disillusionment. The radical novelty of Jesus Christ does not break the connecting link between initial human faith and faith in him, for the latter is the restoration, exaltation, and salvation of the former.

Every human being starts out with some faith-inspired intuition, but everyday experience tends to undermine and destroy it as time goes on. The course of life seems to prove the uselessness of every effort on behalf of liberation. Egotism and injustice seems to reign supreme, as the lamentations of the prophetic and sapiential books of the Old Testament indicate. The death of Jesus was the clearest proof, it would seem, that people of faith had entertained delusions for centuries. But the presence of the living and active Christ, attested to by his apostles, is a revelation that in Christ we are stronger than any delusive appearances. That is how faith is salvaged and we are saved.

Faith gives rise to active charity, which in turn prompts a bold struggle against the evil rooted in the world. The fact is that human activities are not neutral. Viewed in the abstract, technologies, sciences, and industries clearly have nothing to do with faith or with humanity. But that situation changes as soon as they are applied to specific tasks, for then they operate in the context of a social system, a value system, and a personality structure. Thus they will tend to reinforce or to alter these systems and structures. They will serve either egotistical interests or community interests, our drive for oppressive domination of others or our drive for charity and true service to society. Charity operates in and through the instruments available in a given civilization, and it even helps to foster and promote those instruments. At the same time, however, it is the end result of a conversion wrought in the individual and on society; it places all the instruments available in the service of emancipation rather than in the service of oppressive forces.

Charity is a victory over the established situation on every level. It is the anticipation of a future that does not yet exist and the active will to create that future. So charity is based on hope, the hope of being able to alter human beings as individual and social animals. And hope in turn is based on faith in the power given to us, faith in the Spirit who has been sent to bring something new into being.

Lack of charity presupposes a lack of hope, and lack of hope presupposes a lack of faith. Abandoned to ourselves, we readily give way to resignation and adapt to the established situation. We lose faith in ourselves or faith in God, which really is the same thing because faith in self is faith in the God who gave us the power to act and attain salvation.

Hence if we consider salvation in terms of its presence

in us, if we view it as an effect produced in us and a way of being human, then we can say that it is the salvation of faith. We had lost faith in our destiny and in the possibility of ever attaining it. We were wandering aimlessly when Christ came along. Christ restored our confidence in the destiny of the human individual and the human community. He also confirmed and broadened it, giving it a clarity and perfection it never had before in the history of humanity. Jesus' life, death, and resurrection as well as the coming of the Spirit to the Church —evident in numerous signs—constitute motives for faith that are radically superior to all that existed before them.

To save us means ultimately to save whatever it is inside us that is the wellspring of our initiatives, our projects, our options, our creative dreams, and our perseverance in adversity. It means to save our faith in human effort and in ourselves by revealing to us its inexhaustible source in a creating God who is the God of freedom rather than of bondage.

The concept of salvation signifies that faith, hope, and charity are not wholly novel realities appearing on the scene with Christianity. Christian faith is the age-old human faith of people in their humanity, a humanity that had been wounded and diminished by sin, but that now has been restored to an unexpectedly full measure. Christian hope is the age-old human hope in the heart of every person; it too has been reinvigorated and grounded on solid arguments. Christian charity is the love burning in the heart of every person, a love that is now rekindled and brought to its fullness by the power of the Spirit.

7. Gospel Mission as Service

The whole theme of service was brought into sharp focus by Vatican II, and it has been bandied about by everyone since then. It is given all sorts of different connotations and is used in all sorts of different contexts. So we must spell out clearly what exactly is the service to be performed by the Gospel missionary.

First of all we must realize that salvation has nothing to do with a prefabricated or ready-made salvation that is already set up in a structured way. We cannot just walk into some structure and thereby be saved. Unfortunately many Catholics see the Church as such a locale of salvation. They think it is enough to enter the Church and stay firmly attached to it in order to be assured of salvation. In such a perspective, then, the work of the missionary is to get people to enter the ecclesial structure and remain faithful to it; salvation will flow naturally from there. It is a sure thing entailing no risks or problems. The Church is a religious institution guaranteeing salvation and leading people to Christ in an uncomplicated, natural way.

The fact is, however, that the Church by itself cannot save anyone. As a human society with its own line of thinking and reflection and with its own brand of pastoral activity, the Church cannot plot and carry out the task of saving human beings without their involvement. It cannot present them with a prefabricated salvation plan that does not enlist their own active involvement in it. It is becoming clearer every day that the Church does not possess any ready-made solutions, that on its own initiative and by itself it cannot effect liberation, justice, and love here among people. The Church does not possess any revelation telling it how to act concretely in order to bring beings to salvation and freedom. It has no plan for societal life or personality development.

Missionaries must give up the presumptuous notion that they can give salvation to human beings. Proceeding from sentiments of pity and compassion, this notion is the temptation of the Grand Inquisitor in Dostoyevsky's novel. That character tolerates evil and wrongdoing in human beings and wishes to give them salvation. They, however, do not want to accept the gift. The Grand Inquisitor, and any like-minded person, must therefore impose a salvation on people that they themselves do not particularly want. It is the same with violent revolutions, which end up imposing a freedom that people do not want and thus creating a new tyranny in the name of freedom. Over the centuries the clergy have exercised tyranny over human consciences, and they have even gone so far as to use the secular arm to impose a salvation that people would not freely accept. Thus the will to save human beings ends up losing them, for they are placed in a state of bondage where they eventually lose even the desire for salvation.

The fact is that the Church did not receive any capability of effecting salvation for human beings, much less of imposing some salvation on them without their involvement. The ambitious will to save people in spite of themselves is a carryover from the realm of politics and government authority. Political authority certainly does have the task of maintaining some form of order and peace between people, but power itself always remains ambivalent. While it is entrusted with the task of establishing justice, freedom, equality, and human dignity, it always ends up being transformed into new structures of oppression. Power centers are not superhuman. They are no more prone to justice than the average human being is. It is illusory to think that we can save human beings by offering them some new prefabricated structure. In and by itself no structure can give freedom to human beings. No structures can provide love unless there are human beings around who are willing to show love.

That does not mean that structural reform is useless, however; quite the opposite is true. There can be no justice or charity without structural reforms, but such reforms must always be rooted in people's willingness to exercise freedom and love. Insofar as structures are dependent on some power center, they will tend to become instruments of domination wielded by that power center. Thus the actions of those in political power will always be limited, ambiguous, and capable of fomenting liberty and tyranny at the same time. Political power must always be watched carefully.

Christianity is concerned with this very problem. It seeks to make sure that human beings will always keep control over the machinery of government and retain power in their own hands. Christ must win out over all power centers and keep them under his control. Power ensures justice only when human beings can maintain control over its exercise. Of itself it cannot provide salvation. It is salvific only if it is responsive to saved human beings. In themselves power and authority are designed to maintain some degree of external order, not to create justice.

In the hands of the Church power offers no more

security or guarantees. Instead it corrupts the Church itself. For centuries the Church tried to enlist the power of the state in the cause of evangelization and evoked great resistance as a result. So great was the resultant mistrust and scorn and hatred that today the Gospel mission must try to break down a host of resentful feelings in order to reach the hearts of those who live outside the confines of the Church.

The salvation of human beings must begin in the heart of a human being. The Spirit is given to human beings, not to the Church so that it may transmit the Spirit to them. Through social channels the Spirit is given directly to the individual, and human liberation is the result of a movement that is born inside the person. We are not abandoned to ourselves. Salvation comes to us from the Spirit of Jesus Christ, but this Spirit does not operate as some principle located outside or alongside us. The Spirit operates as a force within us, and the relationship is so intimate that we may not even be aware of the Spirit's presence. Indeed people may live their whole life under the inspiration of the Spirit without ever being cognizant of the Spirit's presence. For only the word of the missionary can make that presence known.

To attain salvation we are not called upon to leave ourselves; we are called upon to return to the very core of ourselves, to the wellsprings of our being and our humanness. We are not asked to submit ourselves to some alienating thing outside that will force us into a dependent relationship. Salvation is imbedded in our very hearts by the Creator, and this is made manifest in and through the gift of the Spirit.

It often happens that people are driven in desperation to look for salvation in some sort of flight or haven of refuge. Many religions offer people a haven where they can forget their obligation to be human, where they can toy with fantasies and content themselves with serving the gods or the spirits. It is a form of alienation, but it offers security, peace of mind, and inner peace—which people tend to appreciate more highly than freedom and love.

But if it is true that salvation and the mission of the Church are not concerned with offering some salvific realm or some clearly marked pathway, how can they be of service to the world? How do they serve human beings?

As we just noted, a Gospel mission catering to our escapist inclinations might well be more certain of success. Missionaries might well be more successful if they preached a false notion of Christianity. But we are interested in submitting to the demands of authentic Christianity, and so we must look at the Gospel and see how Jesus operated. What was the scope and purpose and praxis of his mission? Since it would be impossible to summarize all the data provided by the Gospels and by biblical theology, we must be satisfied with focusing on the basics here.

The missionary activity of Jesus involved two fundamental actions: proclamation and exhortation. His proclamation centered around the arrival of the kingdom (or reign) of God, and it was carried out with spoken words and sign-pointing gestures. His words and signs told people that the kingdom would not take any form compatible with the prevailing messianic notions of the day. It would not be embodied in some outside state of affairs external to people themselves. The kingdom arrives inside people, entailing a change in the human individual. All of Jesus' signs point to this rebirth: the blind see, the deaf hear, the crippled walk, the dead are resurrected, and so forth. We are obviously dealing with some principle of life that is reawakening in people. They had been sick and paralyzed and somehow dead; now they suddenly are capable of full life once again. It had been impossible for them to act as human beings; now their humanity is suddenly brought back to life. Jesus' discourses make the same point, i.e., that the kingdom is an inner rather than an outer reality. Saint Paul makes the same point in somewhat more abstract terms, talking about the death of the "old man" and the birth of the "new man." Saint John describes the same reality in terms of "light" and "life."

The second basic action of Jesus was exhortation. Jesus issued a summons to human beings, urging them to bring their lives into conformity with the kingdom of God. We ourselves must flesh out and live the process which the Spirit has initiated within us. The activity of the Spirit and the activity of people are not two activities but one and the same activity. Jesus' summons is directed to the very heart of us, to the core of humanity that lies buried in every human being. It presupposes and derives from a real confidence in that core, in our capacity for change. The summons is not a threat, an obligation, an orientation. For every new action that is performed by renewed human beings derives from within them, from people who have been accosted and summoned. It is not a matter of directing or controlling them. Conversion is necessarily a personal action, a personal response to the summons. It must be repeated and renewed day after day once the human individual has made the basic decision to root out the last traces of sin and egotism and the will to dominate. Jesus presents his wisdom as a summons, and then he waits for our response.

Christianity, then, presupposes that some form of external summons is necessary. The summons does come from outside, and only in that sense can we say that salvation comes from outside. Salvation is not a prefabricated totality existing outside us, but it is someone outside calling to the individual. That is precisely

how Christianity differs from self-enclosed systems and
ideologies. It is grounded on the summons of one human
being issued to another human being, and that summons takes the form of service; love of neighbor is the
service that embodies the summons. Thus Christian salvation does not spring from human beings who are
closed up in themselves; it springs from human beings
who are open to others, and the whole process is initiated by Christ himself. Christian salvation begins with
one person's act of love for another person. Self-
reflection will never bring us to salvation. Someone must
approach us and summon us, to awaken the humanity
that lies dormant within us.

Jesus showed his love for human beings by speaking
to them and trying to rouse the authentic humanity
within them. He did not allow himself to be cowed by the
resistance of people, of society, and of the established
structures. He kept speaking and acting until he was
totally rejected and persecuted even unto death. That
was the service he rendered to human beings, and it is
carried on in the Gospel mission, which is one of the
instruments of the service rendered by Christ. We all
need the love of another in order to attain salvation. We
cannot be saved by our own initiative; we must be summoned by another.

The summons of Jesus Christ can reach people
through many different channels. Something of this
summons has resounded in human hearts since the very
first days of the human species. The mediators were
other people, who may not have even realized that they
were acting as instruments. Personal experience itself
shows us that there are always other people in our lives,
that the spoken word of others is the stimulus that
awakens us. We are never roused solely in and by ourselves. Salvation is immanent and transcendent at the
same time. It is transcendent because the response to

that summons comes wholly from the person who is addressed by it. The Spirit is not a third party who steps in alongside two other parties; instead the Spirit is at work inside the two people who are engaged in dialogue.

The missionaries of Jesus Christ are obedient to a mission that they fully and consciously accept. What people had been doing in a groping, imperfect way now comes into its own. Service reaches its maturity at last. Now the missionaries must transmit the word of Jesus Christ to others, that is to say, must make the proclamation and exhortation of Jesus Christ present for concrete human beings in concrete situations.

If missionaries are to be present to others as ones who offer help and service, then they must get close enough to have real access to others. Such access is not easy to come by, however, precisely because others are "other." Even the closeness of certain social relationships does not facilitate the matter. One might imagine that parents, brothers and sisters, neighbors, and fellow workers would make the best missionaries, but the fact is that we are never prophets in our own country. The relationships of family, neighborhood, and everyday contacts tend to transmit a culture, a religion, and a system of security rather than the Gospel message itself. If the Gospel is to be transmitted through the ordinary channels of social intercourse, then the people involved will have to prescind from those basic social ties to a large extent. The process of evangelization will always entail the overcoming of obstacles and barriers, for it involves the encounter of one "other" with a second "other."

If missionaries are to be capable of truly encountering the other person, they must be capable of prescinding from their own culture. They must be able to simplify their language and their approach, to strip down their attitudes and words and gestures as much as possible.

Theology is not just of little use in transmitting the message; it is actually a serious obstacle. One must be able to express the Gospel message in the most universal terms possible, using the most common words possible. The first and foremost function of any theology should be to enable us to prescind completely from it. We can never remove ourselves completely from the culture in which we received and worked out the message of salvation and faith, but missionaries must do all they can to detach themselves from that culture as much as possible.

This applies not only to the spoken word but also to the language of gestures and actions. The message of salvation operates in and through characteristic signs or gestures that bear visible witness to God's presence and the existence of a human salvation.

What is more, emissaries of Jesus Christ must be familiar with the language of the others if they are to be able to initiate a dialogue. The language of the interlocutor is no more capable than one's own language of containing the whole of salvation. It will always be necessary to perceive the true import of what is said in and through the signs offered. Missionary service, then, will entail seeking and using signs that express something about the kingdom in terms that are comprehensible to the other person. The message of Jesus Christ cannot be presented abruptly—that is, without some sort of sign or language that is comprehensible to the listener. Missionaries study and assimilate the culture of their listeners to the point where they can present them with real signs. They really cannot offer anything more than signals, and Christ himself speaks through his Spirit amid them.

Both the culture of the missionaries and that of their listeners can be obstacles to the transmission of Christ's message. In the case of Jesus himself, the Jews confused the signs with the spoken message. They equated the signs of the kingdom with the kingdom itself, and this ambiguity will always be present. Human beings will always be inclined to expect some sort of salvation from the missionaries themselves instead of realizing that they themselves must assume responsibility for effecting it.

Since missionary activity is nothing more than a summons, there is no guarantee that it will be effective in any concrete case. The missionary knows that the message is effective as a general rule but does not know exactly how it makes its way into people, grows within them, and bears fruit. If people do not respond to it, it is difficult to say whether its ineffectiveness is due to a failure in the communication process or an outright rejection of the message and salvation. Even in the worst cases one may still suspect that the message was not really communicated. We can never be absolutely sure that a person has firmly and finally rejected the salvific word of Jesus Christ.

Insofar as the recipient is concerned, conversion is always a slow and gradual process. It takes many twists and turns, and it goes on till death. Missionaries have no right to expect a specific concrete response or a well-defined level of faith and charity. They live wholly dependent on the people they are seeking to evangelize. Placed in their hands, missionaries can only follow their footsteps and stay tuned to their own rhythm and pace. They cannot oblige the people to follow some prearranged route, to get rid of all their sins at once, or to operate according to some pre-established set of priorities. Conversion will never be a finished process. We tend to feel that we are more converted than other people only because we are more aware of their sins than our own. The Gospel mission obliges us to change this spontaneous attitude.

What must be stressed in any case is the fact that the summons of Jesus Christ cannot be reduced to any human culture. If his apostles are satisfied with simply expressing his message in some form that is perfectly adapted to the categories and cultural forms of their listeners, then they will never be able to reach the inner core of humanness that lies buried in the individual. They will never touch the person's basic humanity that lies buried under all the trappings of cultural life. Instead of helping their listeners to make progress, the missionaries will simply offer them a reflection of the surrounding culture. Adaptation is necessary, to be sure, but it merely opens the process of dialogue. The most basic and critical words are spoken at a level of shared humanity where individuals get beyond their personal systems and their social cultures.

Thus the process of conversion applies to both the missionaries and their interlocutors, and it takes place on a human level where people divest themselves of their cultural certainties and their security systems and approach each other as human beings. At that basic human level things are not carefully structured and defined. Human beings meet each other in mutual respect and in a common quest for truth. The service performed by Jesus Christ and every missionary is to bring another person to that level.

8. Gospel Mission as Strength in Weakness

No one has stressed the fragility and weakness of the missionary more than Paul. The apostle of Christ seems to face insurmountable obstacles: the resistance of other people, the hostility of authorities, the challenge of physical barriers, and his own deficiencies of mind and body. Paul, more than anyone else, has underlined the great disproportion between the goals sought by missionaries and the means at their disposal, between the scope of their task and the ridiculous flimsiness of their tools.

Missionaries are not geniuses. Their mission does not require people of an exceptional nature, and missionaries in fact are not extraordinary. At times in past history they have tried to hide their deficiencies under impressive external trappings, but the ruse has not worked. Missionaries cannot rely on such stratagems, for they will fail. When they try to operate in that vein, they end by transmitting a religion, or a culture, or an ideology, rather than Christianity. They simply transmit the culture of the people or nation who provided them with the trappings.

Weakness is no accident in the work of the Gospel mission, nor need it be lamented. On the contrary, it is a necessary precondition for any authentic mission. It finds its justification in the fact that the Son of God appeared without any of the attributes of human power or strength. Jesus did not try to shine by virtue of his education or cultural training. He did not try to present an argument along the lines followed by the doctors of the Jewish law or by pagan philosophers. He did not win people over with impressive charitable works or development schemes. He did not try to impress them with power. The typical messianism of his day was quite alien to him, and the supreme sign he gave to people was his own death. It was a visible manifestation of his complete inability to convince and dominate people by arguments based on the trappings of human cultures and human civilizations.

The fact is that Jesus went about completely unarmed and defenseless among human beings. That is how he wanted to be, for he wished to touch people at the very core of their humanity. He wanted to reach them on the most universal level, to touch the innermost humanity and be accepted by the lowliest. That is why they responded so willingly to him, and why people of wealth and power felt touched at some point beyond the trappings conferred on them by socio-cultural structures. Jesus was unarmed so that he could get at the truth and touch human beings there. Human beings had to drop their masks and reveal what was innermost in themselves. This point is a dominant idea in the Gospel of John.

At the same time, however, Jesus makes clear the complete weakness of unarmed truth in the midst of humanity. He thereby reveals what sin is. If this truth had not been revealed, then any human category could have retained its ambiguity. Lying, cowardice, and injustice could have remained hidden under the cover of social and cultural rationalizations: "It is better . . . to have one man die . . . than to have the whole nation destroyed" (John 11:50). There are countless reasons of that sort which help to justify the atmosphere of lying injustice and homicide in which people are forced to live. The complete helplessness of unarmed truth shows up in the relatively prompt death of Jesus. It did not take long for society to resolve the problem he represented for it.

If Jesus had not been so utterly defenseless, he would not have spoken to the human heart. Instead he would have appealed to the surface level of human life that is a compound of established social and cultural practices. His words would have been prompted by fear, by respect for the strong, by a desire for personal security and safe refuge, and by similar reasons. His preaching would have remained within the bounds that every civilization sets for its people so that they can survive amid injustice and cowardice. His preaching would have been one more element helping to integrate people into the surrounding culture. And that would hold true even if he had urged revolt and rebellion, for such revolt is merely the ultimate step in trying to integrate people into a culture.

The weakness of Jesus is not just an inability to defend himself. It is also an inability to act in any way that might provide an answer to people's problems and questions. Jesus possessed no capability of providing any answer to human problems. He could not resolve political or economic or personal problems. He could not liberate people from the dominating hold of poverty, ignorance, or state power. He lacked the tools of action, the tools possessed by human cultures to work out answers for the challenging problems posed by life. Human beings are always waiting and hoping for someone to come and take away the seemingly intolerable burdens of life. To them Jesus offers nothing but a summons, showing them his own weakness and inviting them to look to the depths of their own humanity for new sources of strength. He does not liberate anyone from the heavy burdens imposed by life.

Jesus is no messiah in the popular sense of the term. Those who were looking for some form of messianic deliverance were soon disillusioned. And every succeeding generation of Christians has experienced the same weakness in its work of evangelization. The world is solidly grounded in ambivalence and wickedness, and Christians seem incapable of budging it. They are fated to suffer persecution and apparent failure. In the short run the failure is very real, and it confounds their hopes.

The resurrection of Jesus, however, proves that the strength of God is to be found in this seemingly total weakness. God's strength is at work in human beings so that they may be capable of a similar resurrection.

The power of God does not operate from the outside, offering ready-made solutions to human problems. The physical miracles of Jesus should not be viewed as the start of an age of miracles. They should be viewed as visible signs of the miracles taking place inside human individuals. God's strength is at work to awaken human beings. Thus the trust and confidence of the missionary is centered around the miracles that the message of Jesus Christ is capable of working inside every human being, thanks to the simultaneous presence of the Spirit of Jesus himself.

Evil is not securely and definitively rooted in the human heart. Human beings are vulnerable, and the possibility of change and conversion is based on that fact. If that were not the case, then human history would be merely a power game between two opposing forces. It would simply be a matter of trying to guess the outcome at any given point on the basis of the existing balance of power or changes in that balance. Human wisdom would have nothing to talk about but the final victory of force and power.

Christianity, however, proclaims the fact of strength in weakness, and its message was foreshadowed by many earlier pronouncements. It proclaims the strength and power of truth, which is grounded on the vulnerability of human beings and the presence in them of God's Spirit, the Spirit of resurrection and life. Only that accounts for the fact that revolutions do not represent merely a change in masters but rather a new stage of increased liberty and fraternity. The strength of the word slowly dissolves the resistance of evil. It eats away at evil persistently and is willing to accept suffering and persecution in the process.

But the temptation to rely on force and strength is a strong one. The missionary, like other human beings, is tempted to seek an alliance with the power of the state and with the resources of a culture. One need only take note of the role accorded to religion and philosophy by any society to realize that fact. The role is there, ready for use, and one need only accept it. It is simply a matter of becoming an integral part of established society, and historical experience shows that an alliance with the power and wealth of a culture pays off handsomely. The Christian cultures of the past bear clear witness to the effectiveness of the resources that society places at the disposal of its religions. The Church benefits greatly by coming to an understanding with the established system and its authorities. It is duly honored and well treated, and its membership grows greatly. Its ministers are treated as important people by society. The power of human resources can pay off well.

But a nagging question remains: What are the ultimate fruits of this integration into human society and this utilization of its resources? It is certainly true that the salvation brought by Jesus Christ includes the subordination of all worldly forces to him. All the facets of human activity and their fruits are to be recapitulated in Christ. But the fulfillment of this goal will come only at the end of the Gospel mission, not before then. The danger is that the powers of this world will rebel against the rule of Christ and place it in their own service. It is not a vague possibility but a constantly recurring fact in history. What this means in practice is that the Gospel message and the activity of the Church are reduced to the role of helping to integrate people into a given society and culture.

Instead of commanding, then, the word of Jesus Christ is reduced to bondage and plays the role of the Second Beast in the book of Revelation (Rev. 13:11ff.). The First Beast represents the powers of this world. The Second Beast symbolizes the false prophets who teach people to accept the established order and to submit to the existing power structure. Missionaries betray the Gospel mission when they place it in the service of some established culture and accept a well-defined role within that culture. The message then becomes inoffensive and totally inoperable, and Christianity becomes just another cultural element. It may still serve as a noble factor in human history, but it no longer serves the salvation of humanity. The salvation it preaches in such a context is a mythical one like that preached by other religions of the same sort. Its heaven is like that of the Muslims, for example. The fact is that a good Muslim will attain heaven just as a good Christian will. There is no great difference in that respect, and both Christian and Muslim theology have taught the same lesson.

When Christianity is thoroughly integrated into a society, the Church enjoys a privileged situation. It is one of the organs of the state alongside such organs as the army, the school system, and the bureaucracy. It enjoys stability and prosperity, but its message no longer gets to the core of people.

This temptation has existed from the very beginning and it will always continue to exist. It is one of the constants in Christian history. Thus the Church is summoned to an ongoing process of conversion, and missionaries are persistently summoned to recapture the authentic nature of their mission and salvage it from the corruption that threatens it. All the great missionaries were people who gave new life and impetus to the Gospel mission. In all the great epochs of church history people felt obliged to rediscover the true nature of the Gospel mission and to salvage it from various distortions. At bottom the potential distortions remain the same, and the Church is constantly summoned to conversion. The object of conversion remains the same too. The potential danger is that the Church will become too integral a part of a given society, that it will renounce the Gospel mission and accept a subordinate role in the prevailing culture. The work of the Gospel mission begins with the liberation of the missionaries themselves. They must free themselves from all the sources of strength accumulated over centuries so that they can once again discover the weakness of Jesus Christ.

Missionaries face the same temptation that was faced by Jesus: the temptation of messianism. They are tempted to make full use of power, money, authority, and cultural backing. Their intention is always that these be placed in the service of the Gospel, but these forces end up rebelling and winning domination over the evangelization process. The cultural forces always prove to be stronger than the missionaries who plan to use them for their mission, and the Gospel mission itself ends up as a diminished and tainted reality.

The course of history reveals an alternating cycle of stages. At one point the Gospel mission is integrated with a given culture too much, and then it manages to free itself from the attachment. Right now we seem to be in a stage of emancipation and liberation. The Church is slowly and painfully returning to its proper poverty and weakness as it divests itself of cultural, economic, and political superiority. Some people are lamenting the loss of these resources, even as some Hebrews lamented their departure from Egypt when they were in the Sinai desert. But today as then, one must strip down and pass through the desert before one can carry out a truly Christian mission.

9. Gospel Mission as Witness

In recent years church theology has become aware of the excessively private character that Christianity has taken on since the end of the Middle Ages, and particularly over the past hundred years. There has been a strong reaction against this tendency, and it is growing day by day. The fact is that the message of the Bible is thoroughly social and political. The word of God in the Old and New Testaments is uttered in the marketplace as well as in the depths of an individual's conscience. Jesus spoke out in the open where the Jews of his day walked and congregated. He proclaimed his message along the byways, in the streets of cities and towns, and in the Temple (which was the great meeting place of the Jewish nation). He spoke openly before the authorities of his day in every field: before the religious scholars, the priests and elders, and the Roman rulers. He did not keep his message a confidential secret between himself and certain select groups buried anonymously among the masses. Indeed he might not have provoked a reaction from the authorities if he had chosen that secretive approach. It would have been much simpler and safer to teach his religious doctrines to a small group of discreet and attentive disciples, but Jesus chose a very different course. He spoke his message to the public and went out to confront those in the established centers of power. His message would contradict the traditional wisdom and the existing national structure, but Jesus would not conceal its subversive thrust. In a loud voice he stressed the antagonisms and contradictions existing between his Gospel message and traditional structures and doctrines. The four Gospels highlight the public nature of Jesus' preaching and his mission, and the public nature of the activity of the early Church is highlighted by the Acts of the Apostles and the letters of Paul. Saint John fashions his synthesis around the theme of witness and public testimony, and the book of Revelation presents the drama of Jesus confronting the powers of this world. There is a total and public struggle between the world, armed with the strength of its various structures, and Jesus and his followers who are weak and totally disarmed.

It so happens that sin, the adversary, is not to be found solely in the conscience of the individual human being. It is not simply a matter of trying to effect a will to undergo change in the individual human heart. What we must do, in other words, is realize the full implications of authentic conversion. The sinfulness from which Christianity is trying to save us is a structured reality. The world is submerged in sin on every structural level, be it economic, social, or political. Sin pervades everything so that the choice of sinning or not sinning does not depend on the individual human being. We must commit injustice and tolerate it by virtue of this world's structures. Economic life is so set up that it is not possible to practice justice. Political life is worked out to maintain order in what is essentially an unjust society. The power of the state is placed in the service of unjust and oppressive situations. Education and cultural training are designed to make this sinful situation comprehensible, acceptable, and tolerable. Every possible effort is made to conceal the negative features of society and to highlight the beauties of the established order. People must somehow be convinced to accept things as they are. If we do want to practice justice, then we must flee society. Wasn't that the underlying reason behind the rise of the monastic life and the inner meaning of the desert?

It is not enough to say that a human being is saved by good intentions, that good intentions will suffice if one cannot possibly practice justice. If that were true, then the salvation brought by Jesus would simply come down to sowing the seed of good intentions without reaping any effects in reality. No such idea appears in the Bible. His work of salvation is a real effort to effectively save humanity. Hence it becomes imperative to know the nature of the sinful structures and the forces which help to incorporate us into them. Witness, then, is public testimony designed to confront and eventually overcome the sinful structures that keep us collectively imprisoned by evil. It is addressed to people who live an organized life in this world. But how can witness challenge the world's sinful structures?

What exactly are the sinful structures that dominate us and keep us enmeshed in sin? They are not structures wholly external to us, for then we could free ourselves simply by removing them. Nor are they simply institutions, though they may give rise to institutions. The institutions that embody our domination of each other arise and perdure because human beings, all human beings, are accomplices in the fact. Some human beings step in to play the role of oppressor or dominating party; others play along by accepting and confirming that role; still others seek to replace those now playing the role. It is not just a few people who are bad. Everyone collaborates in one way or another—some by their egotism and others by their cowardice, some by aggressiveness and others by their fearfulness. The institutions of injustice exist within each human being; they would not last for a day if people were not willing to let them continue. Hence sinful structures must be overcome inside human beings. They cannot be separated from us. The structures of sin do not exist outside the people who maintain them; and the institutions perdure, thanks to the support of those sinful structures.

Sinful structures are not maintained solely and simply by a few individuals or a few groups; nor are they maintained by one class. For example, capitalism exists because it has roots in every social class and every group, because it represents a structure that all maintain and support. It will not do to drive out one group if a similar or worse group is ready to take its place within the very same structures of domination.

We are not isolated individuals. In isolation we cannot really exist at all. We cannot do anything, think anything, will anything. We are social, and our injustice is social. Conversion is real and authentic only if it is the conversion of human beings in all our social reality and our impact on the public sphere. The conversion of the individual, if it is an authentically human conversion, injects a dissolving leaven into sin-laden structures; otherwise it is simply a matter of conscious awareness on some superficial level.

The worst sort of ambivalence arises when we attempt to take the structures existing in established institutions and place them in the service of Christ. Institutions fashioned to sustain and support injustice simply will not be of use in trying to implant justice. New institutions are necessary. The individual conversion of heads of state means little in this connection. The witness of Jesus was not directed against individuals such as Pilate but against the Roman system. The book of Revelation was not directed against Domitian, but against the

Roman system as a whole and the complex of sin-laden structures existing in every cultural system. The conversion of an individual leader does not change anything if the whole human group has not undergone a change. The consecration of a people or a nation is ridiculous if it simply means that existing structures and institutions supposedly acknowledge the sovereignty of Jesus Christ. There must be a radical conversion of humanity. Humanity must be emancipated from the structures that now dominate it. The sovereignty of Jesus Christ has to do with the emancipation and freedom of his people.

What are the stages in this process of emancipation? It always begins with the emancipation of a handful of people who become free. Jesus, for example, liberated his disciples from the structures of Judaism and paganism. They became free vis-à-vis Caesar and the Mosaic Law, the Jewish authorities and the Temple. The need for all that disappeared, and the movement spread from this group of freedmen as it does in every era of Christian living. The freedom involved here is not simply a refusal to be dependent on certain externals; it is an emancipation from the spirit of complicity and the forces that tend to make us accomplices in the domination that surrounds us. The small group of disciples around Jesus cut the ties that bound them to sin-laden structures and made them accomplices. The disciples were not converted to live an interior life but to bear witness before a world that was oppressing them and all other human beings. An authentically human conversion is not designed to foster some private form of individual living. We are social beings, and our conduct depends on the structures in which we live. Doing good presupposes and calls for a transformation of all the structures of human life.

Starting with a nucleus of free people, the force of witness spreads. Structures are not inert, nor are they indestructible. If they exist in people, then they can change even as people do. Indeed they can change along with people. All great revolutions arise and develop in the hearts of human beings before they become an established fact in the outside world. They are made up of thousands and millions of individual actions pointed in the same general direction, although their convergence may not be apparent to the superficial viewer. Lacking that kind of support, revolutions merely change one system of domination for another. Authentic revolutions replace institutions that foster domination and exploitation with institutions that guarantee freedom and summon human beings to mutual love. Thus the replacement of institutions is meaningless if it is not rooted in the hearts of human beings. True revolutions grow to maturity through patience and perseverance, through suffering and persecution.

In the concrete vicissitudes of history such transformations are not able to rid themselves of ambivalence. Every worldly transformation has been accompanied by various phenomena of injustice. No group or party is just; the churches do not practice justice perfectly. Conversion always remains incomplete, and the will to freedom is followed by the will to power. Revolution is successful if people's will to freedom proves to be stronger than the will to power of the leaders. When all is said and done, the fact remains that the Christian message is not meant to stay peacefully ensconced in people's souls. It is to make its way into public life.

Witness is the great weapon of the unarmed. It confronts sinful structures with nothing but the force of the word, seeking to root out those structures from the minds and hearts of human beings. Its rivals are those people and groups who propose to offer freedom and justice as if these things were gifts to be given away, who seem to forget that enslavement is rooted in people's will and cowardice. Witness is grounded on the belief that it is possible to change and that only human beings can change structures and force the powers of oppression into submission. If capitalism has roots in all people, a change in the leadership will not accomplish anything. It will simply replace one system of domination with another. We ourselves must be changed. Or perhaps it would be better to say that we must be summoned to shoulder our own liberation and work for it. Every form of freedom has been won in that manner.

Witness enables Christianity to be a creative artisan of history. If it were merely a message pondered in the heart of an individual and applied to private life, Christianity would not engender any history. It would merely be the repetition of the same hidden happenings, forever hidden from view and historically unproductive. But in fact there is a Christian history, and it is the result of the confrontation between witness and the world.

The message of Jesus Christ cannot approach and tackle all the aspects of the world simultaneously. Its approach to the world entails a succession of historical stages, and this gives rise to the history of Christianity. Being a Christian is not exactly the same in different centuries. We are not Christians all by ourselves; we are not Christians outside time. We all undertake our witness within a particular historical era. We are not just numbers in the human race; we are part of an evolutionary process. Being a human today is not the same as it was centuries ago.

For several centuries Christian witness had to confront the ideological machinery of the Roman empire. That machinery paralyzed all activity on behalf of liberty because it enslaved the deepest part of people, their thought processes. People had to overcome the pagan gods and the mythological systems in order to be able to approach the human world in freedom. For centuries

Christians did nothing else but get used to the idea of living independently of the old gods who had paralyzed creatures in their totality. That task is essentially finished today, although we have not emancipated ourselves yet from all the vestiges of that past world. The battle has been won basically, and it will not be necessary to go through that particular stage again. The enslavement of the human mind by mythologies is impossible.

But that was only one stage in the struggle against the powers of this world. Once the world was liberated from the gods, it appeared as it truly is in its social makeup. Individual freedom was attained by the destruction of caste privileges and the emancipation of slaves and serfs. It took many centuries before people came to recognize and acknowledge the notion of the person as a subject of rights, the notion of individual freedom. But there is little progress to be gained by such recognition if the labor system leaves the notion of individual freedom devoid of any solid substance, and that is where we find ourselves at present.

In short, the powers of this world come to light slowly and gradually. The field of combat shifts, and the destruction of certain powers reveals the existence of others that must still be tackled. The witness of Jesus Christ gradually seeps down into us, encouraging us to use the strength of the Spirit to take on the task of our own salvation in all its dimensions. Hence the Gospel mission does not have the same concrete object in every age. To people living today the conduct of missionaries in a bygone day sometimes seems very odd and even incomprehensible. It would be anachronistic to imitate them here and now. We cannot adopt the thinking of Saint Francis Xavier or Saint Francis of Assisi; we cannot act just as they did. If we did, our thoughts and actions would be ineffectual, bringing salvation to no one.

The Gospel mission is historical. The concrete activity

of the missionary is not the repetition of some older model but the invention of a model that will bring out the relevance of the message to today's world. It is not a matter of confronting some abstract or unreal sin of a purely interior sort; it is a matter of confronting real-life sin in all the forms it takes today. Domination, exploitation, and injustice have their own distinctive names today. Today's world has its own character, and today's human beings are specific individuals.

Gospel witness is a word, a spoken message. It is the weakest and most impoverished kind of action. It is the weapon of a ridiculous band of people today, just as it was the weapon of the poor fishermen of Galilee. Missionaries cannot point out the right road to take; they have no solutions to offer. They simply believe people are capable of creating sound solutions, that they do not lack intelligence or resources but rather the will to be free. Missionaries want us to free ourselves from the world that dominates all of us, both the oppressors and the oppressed.

Prophets are threatened with isolation and persecution, and they feel insecure in the face of an uncertain future. It is not surprising that prophets and apostles might be tempted to seek refuge in the calm precincts of an interior religion that looked to another world for salvation. Jesus' own disciples were so tempted, and so are we. They did not want him to go up to Jerusalem and challenge the powers. He could be fairly safe in Galilee, for there was no great danger in preaching a religion that differed somewhat from the authorized Jewish religion. Jesus was persecuted in the end because his message challenged the sinful structures of the world as a whole, including the total religious and sapiential system of both the Jews and the pagan world.

So it will be forever. Christians will not be persecuted for celebrating certain rites. They will be persecuted for facing up to an established system which is suddenly summoned to conversion and reacts defensively. If we look back over the history of the Gospel mission, we will soon realize that we are still at the starting point. We cannot even see where its final limits lie. What has already been done seems very meager by comparison with what remains to be done. But that does not really matter, for history begins anew with each succeeding generation. It does not start from scratch, but from the situation left to us by those who have gone before, however ambiguous it may be. There is no other way.

PART TWO

THE HISTORICITY OF
THE GOSPEL MISSION

No human reality is immutable. In all its human aspects the Church is subject to the law of historicity; it too undergoes change. Twentieth-century theology introduced the notion of historicity into ecclesiology and has tried to comprehend the temporal rhythm of the Church. In what sense and to what extent does the Church change? What factors provoke change in the Church? What possible relationships exist between the evolution of the world and the evolution of the Church?

To tell the truth, however, we must admit that so far theology has not done much to work out the whole problem of the historicity of the Church. The fact of historicity has been recognized, and a few observations have been made on it. That is about as far as we have gone.

Since it is the work of the Church, the Gospel mission is also historical. It, too, changes in time. We can assume a priori that the principles that govern the historicity of the Church will also hold true for its mission. What interests us specifically here is the historicity of the Church insofar as it relates to carrying out the Gospel mission.

10. The Church and History

When we approach this whole issue, we soon discover that the prevailing theology interprets the history of the Gospel mission in the light of two basic principles: the principle of integration and the principle of adaptation. Unfortunately both are totally inadequate for dealing with the problem we are considering here. Both are ideological in that they stem from an overvaluation of the Church's existing institutional system on the one hand and of Western civilization on the other hand. Hence both tend to shore up the stability of existing institutions and to reinforce the Westernization of the Church. In this section I shall try to point up the weaknesses of these two principles and to search for the norms that enable us to properly comprehend the historicity of the Gospel mission. Those norms will be found in the authentic documents and sources of Christianity.

First of all, however, let us consider what the principles of integration and adaptation are exactly. The principle of integration was spelled out clearly by Yves Congar.[1] He maintains that in the course of time the Church explicitates its deposit, that this process of explicitation entails the addition of new elements, and that this addition represents a step forward. The essential features of the principle are to be found in the notions of "addition" and "a step forward." If we take this principle as our starting point, then it is obvious that all the new institutions that have been constructed over the course of church history represent positive additions: Any and all new formulas, theologies, rites, concepts, liturgies, laws, and whatever else represent a positive "increment" that explicitates the church deposit and gives it greater force, authenticity, and value. Thanks to these additions, the Church becomes more and more perfect, more and more developed. Basically they represent progress, not in the deposit itself, of course, but in our way of knowing and living out that deposit. These additions came about in various ways, but it does not matter how they were integrated into the whole complex. The point is that they were added somehow, that this addition represents progress, and that the process can be described as one of integration. It is somewhat comparable to what goes on in a living organism, and many authors adopt that very comparison.

In all fairness it should be pointed out that Congar himself readily admits that not every "addition" was really positive, that there were partial lapses and backward steps.[2] But even they do not really reduce the positive thrust of the process of integration. Viewed in terms of the principle of integration, the institutional development of the Church must be regarded as positive and definitive. It is the external, visible manifestation of the power of the Spirit at work in the Church. The Gospel mission, then, is to proclaim to the nations the Gospel message of Jesus Christ that has been brought together and is now manifested in this institutional complex. To be converted to Jesus Christ means to become an integral part of this institutional complex. The Gospel mission is likewise the expansion and extension of the institutional complex that has taken shape in the West over the last twenty centuries. Speaking in general terms, one can say that every accretion over the past twenty centuries represents an organized growth that is valid, authentic, and necessary. To reject it would be to reject the very Church of Jesus Christ. The most that the Church might do by way of concession would be to give neophyte Christians time and space to assimilate all of the institutional complex. Catechumens and newly formed churches are entitled to have certain institutional "imperfections" for awhile. But it is to be expected that in a relatively brief span of time they will attain the same institutional perfection and completeness exemplified by the older churches.

The second principle governing the historicity of the Church's mission is the principle of adaptation. Some years ago it was presented in almost classic terms by André Rétif,[3] and his exposition was regarded as very progressive and avant-garde at the time. The Gospel mission cannot mechanically transfer the whole structure of older Christendom to new nations and peoples. Certain elements cannot be assimilated by them, and such elements would make conversion impossible. Cultural elements, for example, would fall into this category.

The principle of adaptation is not merely opportunistic, however. It is grounded on the constant practice of the Church in the past. When the Church has gone out to new peoples and new cultures, it has substantively assimilated, integrated, and transformed various elements of those peoples and cultures: profane and religious elements in the culture, languages, art, and so forth. Adaptation has meant assimilating everything that was compatible with Christianity so that these new features might serve as means for expressing the Christian faith.

This principle of adaptation, like that of integration, has been likened to the process of organic growth.[4] Like a living organism the Church grows by assimilating external elements into its life and transforming them into its own substance. This second principle also overvalues the established, heavily Westernized institutional complex. The cultures of the peoples being evangelized must be broken down first, and then partially reincorporated within an already existing cultural complex. They are not permitted to grow and develop according to their own inner developmental laws. At best fragments of those cultures will simply be used in the service of a different cultural edifice. One extreme example of this approach is the use of liturgies or paraliturgies by missionaries in Latin America. They intermingled cultural features from Africa, India, China and elsewhere to form these liturgies. But since many of these elements were not really familiar to the natives of America, they could only be attracted by their externals: the rhythm of the music, the colorfulness of the rites, and so forth. Now all that may be legitimate in its proper place, but it is far from indicating a true appreciation of the historicity of the Gospel mission.

The two principles cited above express features of church history that are in fact secondary in importance. They do not embody the real substance of the Church and its mission. So now we must dig out the important realities which lie buried behind those secondary principles. Those basic realities are two: the Spirit and the Gospel mission. Of course the principles of integration and adaptation do not deny those realities. Indeed they claim to uphold them. But the fact remains that they do hide the true significance of the Spirit and the Gospel mission.

Viewed in terms of those two principles, the role of the Holy Spirit in history is to help us make explicit what lies implicit in divine revelation. The Spirit offers guidance to the Church as it goes about its task in history of developing and organizing that which was originally established by Jesus Christ. Thus when the Gospel of John talks about the mission of the Holy Spirit, it is presumably talking about the homogeneous, straight-line development of the Church in time; and the Holy Spirit is charged with this relatively secondary task. The Spirit is supposed to guide the homogeneous development of the deposit of revelation. Thanks to the Spirit, the Church can adapt to all peoples and cultures without any danger to itself or its harmonious development in history.

But that is not the mission of the Holy Spirit according to the New Testament. The Spirit's essential mission is to help Christians discover the authentic Jesus Christ and his truth. Without the Spirit's help the disciples of Jesus would be an easy prey for the tendencies evident among the pagans and the Jews. They would do exactly what the Jews had done with his deeds earlier, that is, they would adhere to the material letter of his message and fail to recognize the underlying truth. The role of the Spirit is not to help us work out a deposit but to help us get at the essentials.

Christianity is not some elaborate doctrine or liturgy, nor is it a corpus of laws and precepts. Christianity is Jesus Christ, and the task confronting Christians in history is to remain faithful to him. How are Christians to remain loyal to his vision and simplicity amid the varied and complicated influences of history? That is where the Spirit comes into the picture. The Spirit's work is not to help us build a complex edifice. It is to help us maintain the simplicity of Jesus and his original message, to keep us from being submerged in the letter of that message or in the riptides of the culture around us. The work of the Spirit in history is to undo the growing complexity, to keep dismantling the appendages of paganism and neo-pharisaism that might be added.

Cultural growth is not the problem that history poses to the Church. The real problem is that the church must keep going back to Jesus Christ amid the hindrances posed by cultural structures. The assured presence of the

Spirit is a force compelling us to keep going back to the simplicity of the original message. The journey of the Church is a continuing rediscovery of Jesus Christ through an ongoing process of simplification. We must keep going back to the essentials and stripping away everything that is not truly connected with Jesus Christ. The work of the Spirit in the Church is to help us do precisely that.

The history of the Church, then, is not at all similar to the growth of a living organism. Growth is not the goal of Christian history. The true aim of church history is that Christ appear ever more clearly and authentically, ever more distinct from everything that is not truly connected with him. Christ is truly operative in the world to the extent that he can be free of the pressures imposed by pagan religions and Jewish formalism, for these two influences make Christianity more highly structured and more complicated.

In a word, then, the work of the Spirit is not to develop the letter of Jesus' message but to bring out the truth underlying that letter. In history Christians must keep rediscovering the novelty of Christianity and keep overcoming the old by means of the new.

The Spirit is very closely bound up with the Gospel mission. The Gospels tell us that the Spirit steps in when the Church bears its witness, when it confronts the world (Matt. 10:20; John 15:26; 16:8). The Acts of the Apostles and the Epistles show us this process working out in concrete history. The Church discovers its true nature when it moves from one human world to another, that is to say, when it undertakes the Gospel mission. Each new stage in consciousness-raising is a new stage in the Gospel mission, for it is then that Christians take cognizance of the radical novelty of their message. The Spirit steps in, forcing the Church to move out from its present boundaries toward the outside world, as we can clearly see in the case of Saint Paul. The Spirit waits for the Church in the outside world, for it is there that the Spirit will reveal to it who Jesus Christ really is.

In Corinth, amid the Greeks, Paul discovered two things: (1) that Jesus Christ needed no help from Judaism; (2) that he, Paul, was still deeply impregnated with the Jewish outlook when he arrived at Corinth. When the Spirit sent Paul to the Greeks, it was not just to evangelize them; it was also to make it possible for Paul himself to see the real heart of his message. If Paul had stayed among Christian communities made up of converted Jews, he would not have acquired the knowledge of Jesus Christ that he obtained among the Greek Christians elsewhere. The Spirit intervened in the process of preaching the Gospel to outsiders, in the actual practice of the Gospel mission.

It was the Spirit who made it clear to the Greeks that faith in Jesus Christ was a living reality, and the Spirit did so without the help of Jewish culture and its instruments. Paul did not reveal this to the Greeks; he learned it from them. The Spirit reveals to the Church through the mediation of new Christians. The Spirit does not reveal new "things," however. On the contrary, the Spirit reveals that many old things are not necessary, that they actually obscure the truth of Jesus Christ. The history of the Gospel mission is designed to free the Church of inauthentic elements, to reveal to it the simple truth of Jesus Christ. From complexity to simplicity: that is the route of the Spirit and the purpose of the Gospel mission.

A static Church loses sight of its reason for being. The system that it elaborates over time obscures its true purpose, and it ends thinking that its reason for existence lies within itself and its organized system. But the authentic Church exists only in the act of carrying out the Gospel mission. The historical stages of its mission work are stages through which the Spirit enables the Church to keep moving towards its true goal and to maintain its authentic reality. Rather than being a process of growth, it is an ongoing search for its true origins and its authentic reality. And the Church must go out of itself to accomplish it. The history of the Gospel mission is not primarily concerned with such accidental features as cultural assimilation and quantitative growth. It is primarily the continuing search of the Church for its true identity, for its authentic self.

Needless to say, past and present experience shows us a process of institutional growth, social adaptation, and doctrinal formulation. But all such phenomena are secondary in the last analysis, and they must be evaluated in terms of the criteria spelled out above to see whether they represent real growth for the real Church.

The Spirit and the Gospel mission are the biblical concepts that shed light on history. Now we must consider how the biblical message helps us to comprehend the actual happenings in which those realities are made manifest. To do this, we shall consider the biblical notion of "the signs of the times."

Notes

1. Yves Congar, *La foi et la théologie* (Tournai: Desclée, 1962), pp. 111–12.
2. Ibid.
3. André Rétif, *La Mission: éléments de théologie et de spiritualité missionaires* (Paris: Mame, 1963), pp. 58–90.
4. Ibid., pp. 70–73.

11.   The Signs
of the Times

The notion of "the signs of the times" began to gain general recognition and acceptance in the awareness of Christians when Vatican II was convened. But we cannot just mouth the words, for different people interpret them differently. Their interpretation is based on the underlying notion of historicity that they entertain.

Just as there are stages in time for the Church, so there are stages in time for the Gospel mission. These temporal stages are visible to some extent, though their ultimate import is known only to God. Certain happenings do help us to pinpoint various stages in the history of the Church and the Gospel mission. And since the history of the Church is essentially the history of the Gospel mission, as we have indicated above, we must try to recognize the temporal stages of this mission through its visible signs.

If people have a purely organic image of church history, they will see the signs of the times in the various opportunities for church expansion and its quantitative growth. The signs of the times will simply be those indicators that suggest that the Church can win new peoples or spread into new sectors of human society. Other people will regard new adaptations by the Church as signs of the times. Faced with some new situation, it assimilates and integrates new features of human reality. Newly noted cultural elements, new ideas, and new structures are signs of the times, helping to provide the Church with new complex forms.

In fact, however, the happenings that mark the succeeding stages of the Gospel mission are those that show the Church taking new steps to go out and meet others. It is in these steps that we find Jesus Christ being manifested in and through the light of the Spirit. Missionaries may well set out with the idea that they are going to teach something, but in fact they are going to learn something. Living in the midst of other peoples, they will be able to discover the truth of Jesus Christ as it is lived in a freer and more vital way by his new disciples. They will discover that they themselves did not really know him at all, for they will have a chance to strip away the outer trappings which they had confused with the message of divine revelation. They will be able to make contact with the Spirit, who lay buried beneath the letter of the message. The Church is given many different opportunities in history to revitalize its life and to "make all things new" as Jesus himself did. It can be "born again" as Jesus urged Nicodemus to be. But these opportunities do not occur every day. At certain privileged times the Spirit summons the Church to move outside itself (see the account of Paul's vision in Acts 16:9).

The signs of the times are the external manifestations of this call issued to Christ's disciples. The ongoing course of the Gospel mission is not blind, nor is it purely intuitive or charismatic. Reasoned observation and thinking have a role to play. The human mind is capable of perceiving certain things that suggest that times are changing and that a further step should be taken. Different moments of time do have their own signs.

Not everyone perceives these signs. Jesus himself

criticized the Pharisees because they were not wise enough to do just that (see Matt. 16:3–4). There is every indication that some people in every age are insensitive to the signs and unable to appreciate the novel situation that has arisen. To them history is nothing but the on-going elaboration of what has already been achieved.

The supreme sign, of course, was Jesus himself. His life, death, and resurrection constituted a sign that the Jews failed to recognize. It is a unique sign, but the Church must make it visible. Within the Church certain people appear who imitate Christ and thus flesh out the sign that Jesus himself was. These imitators of Christ summon the Church to move into the world outside, showing it that the fields are ripe for the harvest. They break new ground for the proclamation of the Gospel message and thus pave the way for the manifestation of Jesus Christ in the Spirit.

The signs of the times cannot simply be material events or objective happenings as such. Such happenings and events do not point up any human reality or any novel change. In themselves they cannot be indicators. External events may prompt the suspicion that something is brewing, that something is about to take place. Any human being can perceive external events, but many go no further than that. They do not see any summons in objective happenings.

The real signs are human actions, human responses to the challenges posed by objective events. Only human beings, through their gestures and actions, can create realities that point out a roadway and a course to be taken. Signs of the times are those gestures and actions that make present the activity of Jesus in a period of transition similar to the one in which he himself lived. We could make an exhaustive study of some real situation without discovering any signs in it. A sociologist or economist might have studied the society of Jesus' day exhaustively without ever seeing that Jesus was the sign of the times. There is always a connection, of course, between material events and the signs. The missionary journeys of Saint Paul depended on the Pax Romana, the existence of sea routes, and the communications system of the Roman empire. But mere study of those factors would not be enough to enable one to understand what happened in the Greco-Roman world because of his missionary journeys. Only people can be signs; only people can give signs.

In their own day, for example, such people as Anthony of the Desert and Basil and Benedict were signs. Francis of Assisi and Dominic and Thomas Aquinas were signs. All these men were intimately bound up with their times and reflected the material conditions of their day. But their sign value is based on the pathways that they opened for the spread of the Gospel message into the world of their day. They managed to highlight the rise of a new Church and the presence of the Spirit. They proclaimed that the authentic Christ was being manifested in a revitalized Church, above and beyond the complex forms and structures in which their contemporaries sought to imprison the Church.

Let us get down to concrete cases and consider the age in which we are now living, for the real worth of any authentic mission theology lies in helping people to comprehend what is going on in their own day. How are we to know whether we are living in a new historical era or merely continuing a stage that already has a long history? How are we to know whether we are on the threshold of some new Gospel mission or not? Are there signs in our times?

Now if we were simply looking for new ways and opportunities to win people to the Church, we would only have to examine the various resources offered by present-day civilization. We would only have to see how the whole system operates, to consider how various ideological systems make use of the resources now at our disposal. If it were simply a matter of adapting the Church to the new conditions that prevail in civilized life, we might be content to do an in-depth study of present-day civilization. We could study its values and its means of expression to find the best way of assimilating and using them to attract people to Christianity.

But our task is really a very different one. "New times" means that we are faced with a new challenge. A "new world" heralds a new Church, a Church free of the complex structures that it had accumulated from the past. "New times" means a new manifestation of Jesus Christ in the midst of new Christians, in and through the power of the Spirit. It also means the liberation of the Church from its past.

Are we in such an era? In themselves material elements offer us no answer to that question. We must find out whether new pathways are truly being opened up. We must see if there are new human beings around, whose actions constitute a summons to a new task of evangelization.

There are no easy or automatic answers to such questions. There is no clear-cut evidence. We can only have presentiments, personal convictions, intuitions, and confidence in certain happenings and persons. And there will always be evidence to the contrary. Recognizing the signs of the times means accepting the risk of giving up many things from the past. If Jesus had taken all the traditions of the Jews into his own message, it would have been easier to win their adherence. But his mission obliged him to set aside that complex heritage they loved so much. Many could not follow him because they were more concerned about preserving that heritage than about seeking the truth.

Today we witness extraordinary changes in the material context of life. To cite just one example, consider the transition from a rural society based on family ties and local neighborhood ties to an urban society based on an almost infinite complex of social interconnections. Once upon a time people lived in an economy that was based on a relatively simple technology and afforded little more than a subsistence level of existence. Now we are moving into an economy based on very complex technologies that can produce material goods that will radically alter the whole context of human life. It does not seem that the old religions can stay alive amid these changes, for the process of secularization goes on uncontrollably. No religious reality is left intact.

What, then, is the significance of all these phenomena for the Gospel mission? Do they have any meaning at all? Do they herald a new mission or not? We cannot deduce the answer from the events themselves. We must look to the signs. Are there signs of a new Gospel mission? Can we perceive human beings whose actions are breaking ground for a new mission?

It seems to me that we can pinpoint such sign-bearing elements. Since this is not the place to deal with this matter exhaustively, I shall merely focus on three points.

The first sign, I think, is the rise of a new Christian community in a new world of the present day. People all over the world are looking for such a new community, and these converging efforts do not seem to be a matter of mere chance. While they may come from different starting points and be unaware of each other they all seem to point in the same direction.

A second sign is the renewed meaning given to Christian poverty as a way of life. In a society where few people were able to live above the level of mere subsistence, poverty was the lot of almost all and wealth was an offense against God. To choose poverty was to flee the temptation of riches. In our highly technological society, however, poverty ceases to be our fated destiny. It results from the monopolistic control of production by the few, who thereby dominate the many. To choose poverty in this situation is to protest against the social system and to call for the exploration of different approaches that will ensure greater equality within a changed social structure. A life of poverty becomes a call for a just society. Here again Christians are arriving at the same basic conclusion from very different starting points.

The third sign is the emergence of the laity, and hence of the common Christian. The present-day models for Christian living are being presented by typical, run-of-the-mill Christians. They do not have Holy Orders or theological formation. They have not professed solemn vows or acquired positions of authority in the church structure. We are not witnessing the foundation of new religious institutes or a rise in priestly vocations, but rather a quest for new ways of living the Christian life as lay people.

Are these truly signs of a new era? I would not dare to try to answer that question here. What I should like to do now is consider three basic features that go into the historicity of the Gospel mission.

PART THREE

FEATURES OF
MISSION HISTORICITY

The three features to be discussed here derive from the Old Testament, which presents us with a history of God's activity in the world. There is good reason for believing that the writings of the Old Testament are something more than a monument to an antiquated past, that they have relevance for us today. The Church of Jesus Christ has sedulously preserved the witness of the Old Testament out of a conviction that it is not merely a book of souvenirs. The feeling of Christians is that the Old Testament enables us to gain a better understanding of the message of Jesus Christ, that it provides us with indispensable keys to this message and its import. Throughout its history the Church has always felt that the Old Testament spoke about Christ and its own vicissitudes in time, and traditional exegesis and theology has been grounded on that assumption.

One of the elements provided by the Old Testament, however, has not been given sufficient attention up to now. The fact is that the Old Testament (and the New Testament as well) presents a history and a process of reflection on that history. God's revelation is presented in the Bible as a history. Therefore shouldn't this picture of divine revelation as history serve as our key to interpreting the history of Christ, of the Church, and of the Gospel mission in every age?

If the answer is yes, then we must focus on the historical principles that the Bible itself stresses. The three major principles we can detect in the Bible, and which will be considered here, are (1) history as a series of successive stages; (2) history as a process of pedagogy and liberation; and (3) history as a dialectic process.

12. Successive Stages of History

The people of God went through successive historical stages: the age of the patriarchs, the age of the Exodus from Egypt and the wanderings in the desert, the age of tribal community and growing national consolidation, the age of exile in Babylonia and subsequent return to Israel, and so forth. Each stage represented a new realization of the same basic substratum or mode. The very same people of the very same God could live through the very same realities successively on different levels or in different degrees.

If we accept the basic distinction between a model and the plane on which that model is actually lived, then we see that the people of Israel passed through different temporal stages. Each stage was marked by a phase of formation, a phase of maturation, and a phase of destruction. Then it all began over again, but not exactly in the same way it had been lived previously. The cycle started over on a different plane. The Hebrew people came out of each stage a bit more purified, a bit freer of alien elements, a bit more in line with their peculiar calling. In the patriarchal age, for example, the God of Abraham and his family is still very similar to the gods of other nomadic peoples. During the period of the Exodus and the wanderings in the Sinai Desert, the transcendent nature of the God of Moses is revealed to them. Later still, the sovereignty of this God over the land of Palestine is proclaimed. And finally Yahweh appears as a God who rules over the whole earth and who is not bound to any one land.

We will find successive stages in the history of all the institutions and credal beliefs of Israel. We find the same reality in all those phases, but it appears in different forms. Each phase or stage presents a rereading of the previous stage, of the perduring model that underlies all the phases. To use the traditional language that comes down to us through Paul, we can say that any given stage is a "type" of the stages yet to come.

The successive course of these historical stages was not determined by any planning or foresight on the part of the Israelites themselves. On the contrary, they tended to resist all the changes. They could not envision a future that was not simply a further consolidation of the situation existing at the moment. Those prophets who predicted the end of one era and the beginning of another were generally persecuted as traitors and rejected. It was God who forced his people to leave one stage and confront another, to leave the past behind and divest themselves of its trappings. God did this by means of historical forces, by means of political happenings that the Israelites felt powerless to control. When the people felt that they were at the mercy of indomitable forces and did not know where they were heading, it was actually God at work preparing a new destiny for them.

Why, then, should there not be stages in the New Testament? For Christ's coming does not overcome history. History goes on after his coming, for that first coming of his was in the nature of seed being sown. It will take a long time for that seed to grow into a tree.

With the message of Jesus there is a radical change in

the direction of history and in the import of its stages. Before Christ the word of God always remained within the people of Israel; hence each successive stage was somehow connected with them. It was the people of Israel who went through a series of changes that bore witness to death on one plane and resurrection to a higher plane. In the New Testament, however, the fact of successive stages effects the very essence of the new economy. In other words, it affects the mission of the Holy Spirit and the Spirit's outpouring. Each new historical stage is a new step for the mission itself. Thus each new historical stage in the life of God's people now coincides with a new effort to go out and meet the world (the lost sheep) and with the foundation of new churches among the pagans.

The new foundations, however, do not really represent the simple expansion of earlier existing institutions; rather, they represent a renewal of the novel reality now at work in the world. The older churches in themselves do not possess the capacity of renewal. Their structures impede our attempt to return to Jesus Christ. Some new foundation must take place if we are to get back to the authentic sources of Christianity. There must be a new Gospel mission and a new understanding of Jesus Christ through a new outpouring of the Spirit.

On the basis of this principle, then, we can see that the Christian mission does not take the form of progressive expansion from some central nucleus. We can witness that sort of revolution in any given age, to be sure, but it is not the key to the carrying out of the Christian mission. Some particular form of Christian living may give rise to a Christian cultural complex that keeps expanding until it reaches certain limits. At that point the Church seems to come up against an insuperable barrier, to get locked into its past. For some reason it cannot get out and make contact with those outside any longer; but it is not due to any lack of resources, as certain naturalistic interpretations would suggest.

When such a state is reached, only the Spirit can do anything about it. The Spirit must step in and break down the barriers, by prompting certain individuals to act. They appear on the scene as signs. They get back to the simplicity of Jesus' Gospel message through contact with other human beings. The Spirit calls them outside the existing boundaries of the Church, but converting peoples and nations is not their fundamental mission. They are called to establish new centers in which a new Church might arise. Thus the Gospel mission develops out of those new centers, giving rise to change in the Church as a whole.

It seems to me that this schema enables us to comprehend something of what is going on today. The Church had reached the point of stagnation and could no longer get beyond the confines of its existing limits. Conversions were no longer taking place, except among peoples who had followed animist religions and were now looking for a more universal religion. (They were ready for Christianity, as it were, and no real mission effort was necessary in many instances.) The Church was maintained by biological reproduction, as was the ancient people of Israel. Evangelization was limited to the education of children born to Christians, and there did not seem to be any need to go beyond the Church's own frontiers. The outside world seemed inaccessible and, most importantly, the Church could not break out of the existing situation on its own. The apostolic movements of the twentieth century (the lay apostolate and Catholic Action, for example) proved to be wholly incapable of carrying out the tasks assigned to them: i.e., to reconstruct the kingdom of Christ in the world. The

Church could no longer grow by expanding its structures beyond the limits they had already reached. Indeed the principal obstacle to further conversions were Christians themselves as specific and well-defined groups in society. People did not really want to become part of these groups, for parish life was repellent to them.

But where do we go from there? The Gospel mission can proceed further only if there is a new movement beyond the existing boundaries of the Church. It is there we must look for a new impetus to the Church, an impetus grounded on a return to the Gospel message and a simplification of the complex accumulations of past centuries.

Such a new mutation in Christianity was heralded to some extent by major changes in secular society. Civilization was undergoing change on a worldwide basis, so that now the mission field comprises the worldwide realm of urban, industrial, technological society. The rise of this new world appeared to be a terrible threat in the eyes of traditional Christian culture; it seemed to be as cataclysmic as the invasion of Nabuchodonosor was to the Israelites in the sixth century B.C. But a cataclysmic event must occur to end one state of history and begin another for God's people. In the sixth century B.C. it was Nabuchodonosor who fashioned the new stage, however. Each new stage, then and now, is the fruit of the Spirit. It is the Spirit who provokes the signs that serve to give direction to newly arising churches. Guided by these signs, new churches appear to pave the way for a new stage in the history of God's people. It is the new centers of church life, not the old established centers of the Church, that give rise to a new stage in church life.

The new stage is not a mere repetition of the past. Formed and shaped by earlier experiences in its life, the Church can now reach out for a higher and better form of life. It can move even further away from the temptations of paganism and Judaism. It can look more surely to the future, rather than giving in to the lure of the Old Testament traits that lie behind it.

Some elements of the pre-Vatican II Church will disappear forever, specifically those that represented concessions to pharisaism and paganism. Today it is generally conceded that the Gospel mission cannot be carried out by force of arms or by social pressure exerted in the name of patriotism or other political considerations. Such means were used for many centuries, and the Church did not really abandon them; rather, they were taken away from it. The Church did not renounce the use of state power on its own.

Today a new Gospel mission is arising, and it prescinds from the use of governmental power and violence. It is the Spirit who really creates new stages in church history, and today most people will admit that a mission endeavor not grounded on state power is more Christian and more effective. A hundred years ago such an admission would probably have been hard to come by.

It is not the first time that the Gospel mission has undergone such a change in outlook and approach. In one sense we can say that the "conversion" of Constantine and the institution of the Constantinian system was the first great change of that sort. Christians inaugurated a new type of mission once the empire became officially Christian. For the first time they discovered the universal scope of Christianity and its import for the whole of human existence. It was with good reason that medieval historians regarded the Constantinian mutation as the true beginning of the New Testament, for it was then that the message of Christ took a place in public life for the first time. The ghetto Church of the earlier period disappeared when Christianity became the official religion of the Roman empire and began to spread over the world as such. The Constantinian phase allowed for a notable expansion of the Church. Fifteen centuries later, however, it seemed that this expansion had reached its limits and could go no further.

During the Constantinian period, the Gospel mission followed the same basic pattern. Basically it came down to announcing "the true religion" to the peoples of the world. They were expected to abandon their "idolatry" and "superstition." This was the outlook that dominated missionary literature, as one can readily see from the contemporary catechisms and the documents issued by the Congregation for the Propagation of the Faith. The basic theme is always the same: Fight against false religions and reach the true religion.

Then suddenly it seemed that this message had somehow died on the vine. It had become an obstacle to the Christian mission, and so it is today when civilization is officially nonreligious. What once had helped to spread the Gospel mission far and wide is now a serious impediment to that same mission.

Now it is apparent that framing and integrating Christianity within the general context of "religion" was really a retreat to paganism in a more or less spiritualized Jewish form. Historical cataclysms were entrusted with the task of destroying something that the Church itself did not have the courage to destroy. New signs and new human beings arose, and the Gospel mission sprang to new life outside the boundaries of cultural Christianity. The new message is not at all the end product of a natural evolution in the Church. On the contrary, it represents a real rupture with the course of the earlier Church. Older structures were to be destroyed or simplified once again in an effort to return to the Gospel message of Christ.

So the stages of the Gospel mission in history are marked by new creations inspired by the Spirit outside the bounds of the older church centers. There the Church itself learns how to get to know Jesus Christ once again. It is taught by new Christians who do not have to go through the structures accumulated in past history in order to gain that knowledge.

13. Pedagogy and Liberation

In his letter to the Galatians Paul points up another principle at work in the history of God's people. It embodies a divine pedagogy (Gal. 3). We find two successive stages in the manifestation of God's kingdom, one operating through a process of divine pedagogy and the other operating by way of liberation.

What is the exact nature of that pedagogy? Here we should not interpret the word in the terms that are familiarly used by the modern field of education. Like the wisdom literature of antiquity, which to some extent rejected the optimism prevalent in present-day pedagogical science, Paul points up the ultimate significance of all education.

Teachers or pedagogues are entrusted with the task of disciplining, instructing, and drawing out their pupils. They do not direct their attention to the freedom of their young charges. Indeed if they were capable of exercising freedom, the teachers would not be necessary. Any system of pedagogy is a system of constraint and obedience, however gentle it may be. The pedagogues use the arguments of authority, physical force, and moral and psychological pressure. They use sensible stimuli to teach and correct their pupils and to train them in customary habits. Lack of freedom on the part of the students and a completely unequal relationship characterize the pedagogical process.

According to the theology of Paul, which summarizes the novel message of the Gospel in abstract form, the whole history of God's people in the Old Testament was a pedagogy, a system of pressure and coercion grounded on fear of the Lord and the argument from authority. The whole system of Judaism consisted in Law, that is, a body of obligatory doctrines, rites, precepts, and institutions. Obedience was the fundamental virtue from which all other virtues derived their import and value. Fearful acceptance of the Law, which was defined by the elders, the priests, and the scribes, was the direct embodiment of authentic fear of the Lord. The Israelites attained salvation through their obedient submission to the Law.

Paul vigorously stresses the novelty of Jesus Christ in terms of that older pedagogy. Jesus liberates human beings from the Judaic system. He announces the arrival of love, of the Father's love for us and our love for the Father. The period of religious repression and divine pedagogy is over, and all systems of pedagogy are not obsolete. Our salvation now comes from the charity that the Spirit is infusing into the hearts of human beings all over the earth; it no longer derives from obedience to a system of laws, dogmas, rites, precepts, and institutions. Paul's letter to the Galatians is the Magna Carta of this new dispensation.

Thus the Christian mission is radically different from all the efforts at propagandizing and cultural diffusion that stronger peoples and nations have practiced. People are not to enter Christianity through the use of physical, moral, or social pressure. No one becomes a disciple of Jesus Christ through physical procreation, family training, or environmental pressures. Faith, that is, the freely proffered adhesion of the individual, is the pathway to

Jesus Christ. It is love and free submission to the Spirit, not obedience to human authorities and institutions, that prompts a person to follow the Gospel message.

The methods and practices of the Gospel mission derive from that base. Missionaries cannot in any way exert pressure on the freedom of those who are listening to them. Any such pressure would destroy the very purpose they are trying to achieve: to arouse faith in their listeners. The communication of Jesus Christ's message is not effected by relying on the prestige of a culture, on wealth or force. It does not appeal to unconscious feelings and forces. It does not appeal to anxiety, the desire for security, or other emotional factors. This particular communication is made openly and frankly by contact between two people who share intelligence and freedom.

Of course, we all are familiar with these basic principles, but we also know very well that it does not turn out that way in most instances. In practice the vast majority of those who call themselves Christians did not arrive at faith by a process of freely proffered adherence to Christ. Instead they inherited this adherence from their family, and it was reinforced by an educational process within the family and outside that was not devoid of pressure elements. The assumption is of course that this process was ratified by a free act when the individual reached the age of maturity. But such an assumption is overly optimistic in all likelihood, because the pressure of psychological, moral, and social factors would seem to play a more important role in winning adherence to the Church.

To verify this suspicion, we need only consider what many Christians make of Christianity. Many of them see it as a system of religious beliefs, rites, and moral precepts maintained by an institution called the Church. Its mission is to be a strict and vigilant pedagogue. So in the minds of many Christians Christianity is exactly the opposite of what it is supposed to be. For them it is equivalent to the old Judaic system. They know nothing about the Gospel's message of liberation or Paul's proclamation of freedom.

How are we to explain this gap between theory and practice insofar as the Gospel mission is concerned? The fact is that the liberation proclaimed by Jesus Christ has only entered its initial stage. It is still partial and incomplete. It is a seed still growing in human hearts. In the initial phase of conversion and newly acquired faith, charity holds sway and the Spirit keeps people's hearts rooted in freedom. The newly arisen churches are fervent, zealous, and self-sacrificing. But this enthusiasm begins to wane as the communities begin to grow and attract more people. After the second or third generation, people begin to lapse back into the old person, to be motivated by anxiety, yearnings for security, and the need to compromise with the sinfulness of the surrounding world. A host of sentiments and aspirations gives rise to a complex system of beliefs, rites, precepts, and authority centers. Christians feel compelled to catalogue and canalize Christianity. Personal and social tranquillity become urgent goals to be won as quickly as possible.

The Acts of the Apostles and the letters of Paul indicate that right from the start the disciples of Jesus felt a need to look to some law for more solid support. Faith seemed to be inadequate for that purpose, and so they spelled out specific rules alongside the reality of Christ himself. Even Paul, who placed such great stress on the freedom of the Christian, was led to settle individual cases and to add practical rules to the Gospel message. In the first half of his letters he tends to proclaim the basic message of the Gospel; but then he goes on to add regulations that are like the old Law, however revised they might be. At one point he will insist that there is no difference between male and female, Jew and Gentile; at another point he will command women to keep silent in church and urge slaves to obey their masters. The famous dispute between Paul and Peter, which was resolved at the Council of Jerusalem (Acts 15; Gal. 2), should not be overdrawn. Paul, too, slips back into Judaism, but not as much as Peter, and on less significant issues. Pedagogy rears its head once again after emancipation and freedom have already been proclaimed. Once again the children of God are turned into obedient pupils and slaves.

Here we encounter a historical process that recurs inevitably within Christianity. After the high point had been reached, after Jesus Christ had proclaimed the freedom of human beings, there is a regression to the pedagogy of an older time. The Church moves away from Christ and returns to Egypt and Jerusalem. Then the Spirit steps in and compels the Church to undergo conversion once again.

Thus Christian history is not merely a process of evolution and straight-line growth. Rather, it is an oscillating history of decadence and renewal, of lapses from Jesus Christ and then a turning back to him. It is the continuing impact of the older pedagogical system that justifies and demands successive stages in church history. The good news preached by Jesus Christ must be reiterated more than once. There is discontinuity in history because periods of new creation and church foundation alternate with periods of pedagogical solidification.

Insofar as the work of the Gospel mission is concerned, pedagogy takes the form of relying on social, moral, and psychological pressure (and perhaps even physical force) to keep people loyal to the Church. While these means may not be able to engender faith, they can be enough to maintain church membership and religious sentiments.

In its initial phase, the Gospel mission is a process of

evangelization. It is addressed to new people that they might form new communities. Soon, however, these new Christians increase in number and get more organized. The process of organization becomes less a process of evangelizing and more a process of solidifying the existing group. Here the old pedagogical approach enters the picture, for Christians begin to use the same means used by other human groups to maintain themselves: the family, the cultural community, various associations, and the state. Church "sociology" becomes a reality, for Christian society is now analogous to any other human society in its procedures.

In the pre-Vatican II Church, and even today still, most Catholics received their faith from a process of "education" rather than from a process of "evangelization." Most of the personnel and the resources of the ecclesiastical institution are set aside for the former task. They are to organize, solidify, and administer the community of traditional Catholics. That task takes priority over the task of coverting new people so that they might form new Christian communities. It is a reversion to the pedagogical process that marked both Judaism and Pharisaism. There is nothing specifically Christian about it at all. Indeed when it is carried out completely enough, the pedagogical approach can obscure Christ's message of liberation. When that happens, the Church ceases to be the Church of Jesus Christ; it goes back to being a synagogue.

We are coming to the end of one stage. The Spirit will not be able to infuse new life into the Church as synagogue without making use of new ecclesial communities. The work of the Gospel mission is to get away from the pedagogical approach, to proclaim the Gospel message to people outside its clutches who have not been misformed by it.

The Gospel mission is a spiritual one. It is not supposed to make use of all the resources that societies have at their disposal in order to ensure their continuity in time and space. Indeed the work of the Spirit is to revitalize the Gospel mission by liberating it from all such obstructing resources. Evangelization rejects such means to return to the defenseless poverty of Jesus Christ. A truly evangelical mission is necessarily poor, and without such a mission the Church cannot revitalize itself.

14. The Pauline Dialectic

In his letters to the Romans and the Ephesians, Paul offers a general theory of history that is even broader than his schema of pedagogy and the notion of successive historical stages, though the two notions dovetail with his broader theory quite well.

Three terms are involved in Paul's theory: paganism (the nations), Judaism (Israel), and Christianity (Christ). He elaborates a vision that sums up the relationship between the history narrated by the Hebrew Bible and the history initiated by Christ. His view of the way in which the three terms are interrelated in history represents the Christian picture of history.

The point of departure for the historical process of salvation is the complex of world peoples, the nations of the world with their different civilizations. Paul's description of them in the second chapter of Romans is frightening: The pagan nations live steeped in sin. From other texts, however, we know that this sinful corruption is not the whole picture. If it were, salvation would not be possible at all, unless it were a total replacement of one world with another. In any case the fact is that salvation does not derive from the pagan nations; rather, they are the object of salvation. They need a stimulus from outside before they can act to work out their own salvation.

The nation of Israel stands over against paganism as the opposite pole. It is in direct opposition to other peoples and nations, and that opposition is embodied in its complete physical separation from other peoples and nations. Israel will not permit communication. It lives its life removed from other nations and rejects all social contact. The vocation of Israel, from the time of Abraham to the age of the Maccabees, is one of separation. It finds clear expression in the dominant themes that form the substance of the Old Testament: escape into the desert and the glorification of desert life; exodus and exile; nomadic life and ceaseless wandering. The God of Israel defines himself in an exclusivist fashion, declaring that there are no other gods beside him. All the laws of Israel are designed to ensure the total isolation of the nation.

It is certainly true that the Israelites took in many cultural elements from neighboring peoples and tried to live a life like that of the surrounding pagan nations. There are more similarities than differences between the political structures created by David, Solomon, and other Israelite kings and the political structures of neighboring nations. But the prophets repeatedly saw in such structures a sign of infidelity to the vocation that Yahweh had bestowed on the nation. In their eyes the authentic Israel of Yahweh was the Israel that would not allow itself to be contaminated by the appeal of integration and adaptation. The prophets upheld the distinctive vocation of Israel, bearing witness to exclusivism and defending the rights of Israel's jealous God.

In the dialectic described by Paul, Israel is not viewed as the visible political reality that can be studied by historians. It is viewed as the Israel of the prophetic message, the Israel that is open to that prophetic message of

isolation. This authentic Israel is the negation of the
pagan nations in every sense. There is no positive content of a distinctive sort in the notion of Israel. It merely
represents a denunciation of the evil in the surrounding
world. It does not offer any model of salvation; it simply
heralds a future liberation. It represents a promise, and
nothing more.

At this point in his presentation Paul points up a
positive element in the Law of Israel. It is not just a
process of pedagogy that negates liberty; it is also a
means whereby the Israelites are preserved from the sins
of the pagans. Thanks to the Mosaic Law, the Israelites
can preserve their prophetic vocation intact. At least they
can still proclaim it to others, even though they themselves may sin (Rom. 2). Insofar as it stands in direct
opposition to the sinfulness of the pagans, then, the
Mosaic Law is a positive force by virtue of its very
negativity.

And so we come to the third term in the equation. It is
Jesus Christ who effects the reconciliation of pagan and
Jew. But this reconciliation is not effected by a series of
compromises between two completely antagonistic parties. Christian reconciliation entails the creation of a third
term capable of taking in all the positive features of both
parties without being contaminated by their negative
features. Insofar as the pagan nations are concerned,
Christ does not ask them to give up all the cultures and
civilizations that paganism has created, nor does he deny
the value of them. He simply asks them to give up their
sinfulness. Insofar as the Jewish nation is concerned,
Jesus approves and reinforces its negation of pagan sinfulness. On the other hand, he rejects its separatist attitude completely.

How is this reconciliation possible? It is possible
through the force and power of the Spirit, who is capable
of transforming both pagans and Jews. It is the Spirit

who can liberate the former from bondage to sin and the latter from bondage to the Law.

Of what real interest is this Pauline dialectic to us today? The fact is that the reconciliation of Jesus Christ is still a seedling. It is still more promise than reality. We still live in a situation that antedates real conciliation, and the conciliatory work of Jesus Christ is far from finished. The dialectic of Christian reconciliation is an ongoing process throughout the history of Christianity.

Dissociation and paganism still exist. Indeed paganism is continually coming back to life within Christian culture itself. From one point of view it could be said that the expansion of the Church in the world represents the integration of earthly cultures into the kingdom of Christ. From another point of view, however, we could just as well say that it represents the integration of the Church into the pagan cultures of this world. Converted peoples and nations bring a heritage of pagan traits into the Church with them, and it does not disappear overnight. Indeed it may prove stronger than any effort to have them absorbed by Christ.

The integration is carried through in order to facilitate the entry of pagans into the Church. But insofar as the pagan masses agree to enter the Church, the heavy weight of pagan traits grows greater among Christians themselves. The intimate fusion of the Church and various elements of popular culture leads to a degradation of Christianity and a sacralization of the sinfulness already established in the culture. Reconciliation in Christ may lead to actual paganization. In a certain real sense that is what happened in the Byzantine empire, in Medieval Christendom, and in the later age of central monarchies in Europe. What seemed to be a Christian society was actually an avatar of paganism.

The paganization of the Church inevitably gives rise to a renewed emphasis on the message of the prophets, the basic themes of the Old Testament, and the attitudes typical of ancient Judaism. Pure and faithful Christians try to preserve their authenticity by removing themselves from among the masses and forming small elite groups. Their will to purity is backed up by a tendency toward separatism and isolation. A reaction in the name of Christianity rises up against cultural Christendom and its pagan traits. The critical function of the prophets is exercised once again in a newly Judaized Church. Living like the Jewish synagogue of old, it develops its own distinctive institutions and avoids contact with the pagan masses.

But this sectarian attitude, this yearning for purity through isolated living, is no longer justified after Christ. It is valid only insofar as it represents a way of preparing to penetrate more deeply into the pagan world. And so the dialectic is renewed once again: negation, reconciliation, new integration into the world. This dialectical process helps us to understand the various ages and stages Christianity goes through. What specifically interests us here, however, is the history of the Gospel mission. So let us see how the dialectic helps us to understand that history.

Strictly speaking, the Gospel mission is a work of reconciliation. Missionaries go out to the peoples of the world to effect worldwide reunion. They leave a more or less closed community, cross its frontiers, and go out to face the risk of the unknown world. Their aim is to effect a higher union between the older church they have left behind and the new churches that will spring up from their spoken message in the outside world.

Certain epochs in the history of Christianity are dominated by a concern for the Gospel mission and by mission activity. They are periods of synthesis that most closely resemble the apostolic age. These epochs tend to follow periods of closure and isolated withdrawal. It is as if the ground were laid for them by the pedagogical process that dominated a prior age of isolation and self-absorption. Suddenly signs of a revitalized Christian message appear in certain figures, and the Church eventually sends out missionaries to spread this message to people still outside its borders.

But the very success of this missionary endeavor leads once again to the process of integration mentioned above. Once again there is a paganization of the Church. It becomes identified and equated with a particular society and a particular culture. It gives up its mission task and concentrates on preserving what it has already won. Then paganization leads to prophetic reaction once again.

It is very difficult for a church to be missionary if it is closed in upon itself and dominated by a harsh and demanding discipline. There may be no lack of willingness, but the very rigidity of the existing structures means that they cannot be readily assimilated by people who were not raised in the same ghetto atmosphere. Ghetto Christianity is too particularized. It is almost impossible for outsiders to distinguish between the Gospel message itself and the legalistic structures under which it is buried. A ghetto era cannot be missionary, but it may well prepare some people for a mission later on.

To what extent can this dialectical schema help us to understand the age in which we are now living? Perhaps we can say that the more recent epochs of cultural Christendom really represented a neopaganization of the Church. It became an integral part of Western culture, and mission work became almost impossible. The victories of the Church were too closely bound up with the political and cultural conquests of an expanding Western civilization. The decline and fall of cultural Christendom is the logical outcome of its total paganization.

This neopaganization was accompanied by a new

surge of prophetic protest and ghettoization. Protestantism, Jansenism, and Ultramontanism represented a new Judaizing of the Church, a return to the synagogue mentality and its emphasis on pedagogy.

If the schema is valid, then we have every right to expect a new missionary era, a new attempt to effect reconciliation in the Spirit and to go out to new people. Thus we are not in any immediate danger of neopaganization. The task we face right now is the formation of a missionary Church. We must create it out of a nonmissionary Church so that we can initiate a new stage in Christ's mission to the world. That will entail a broad and deep consciousness-raising in the present-day Church.

CONCLUSION

If things are as suggested here, it is not surprising that we are witnessing renewed interest in the theology of the Gospel mission. The notion of Gospel mission spelled out in the first part of this book embodies the new awareness of the Church on the threshold of a new missionary phase. The departure from the ghetto goes hand in hand with an emancipation from the pedagogical mentality. The rejection of traditional missionary methods indicates that it is not a matter of returning to some anachronistic past or of prolonging outdated approaches. The mission field, the parties involved, the means to be employed, and our conception of the whole matter indicate that everything has changed.

We are at the start of a mission that certainly does not envision the expansion or extension of Christianity as it is today. Its goal is the establishment of new churches and the revitalization of older churches by them. We are on the threshold of a new way of living the Christian life. The emancipation and liberation of the Christian message seeks to bring about a way of living the Christian message that has never been known before. The traditional structures in which we were brought up are the ghetto structures of a previous age. They are no longer of any use, because they are more a hindrance than a help to the work of the Gospel mission.

Of course no era of mission activity is ultimate and definitive. No achievement takes in the totality of the human world. The new phase in which we are living now will, in all probability, lapse into the same tendencies witnessed in the past. It will give way to cultural integration and paganization, which will inevitably lead to a new ghetto Church. The process will go on for as long as anyone can envision.

Be that as it may, nothing is more important for us than the task of understanding the age in which we ourselves are living. Before we start organizing any pastoral or missionary effort, we must know the exact nature of our age and its own peculiar signs of the times. In that respect one can hardly say that there is unanimity in the present-day Church. We must look to the authentic fonts of Christianity for our inspiration, rather than allowing long-standing mental habits to dominate our thinking. The earth casts its spell over us, and we tend to attribute its alluring features to God. We must be able to distinguish between the impulses of the flesh and the impulses of the Spirit. We must be born again, leaving our preconceptions behind and opening our ears to the call of the Spirit: "Those who have ears to hear, let them hear what the Spirit has to say to the churches."